Morse Code from Heaven

Morse Code

from

Heaven

RUNAIL GIBSON

Printed in the USA by CreateSpace

Edited by Jean Headley
Typesetting by *www.wordzworth.com*
Cover Design by *www.wordzworth.com*

PROLOGUE

The pastor ended the sermon with, "May God be with you." The church congregation gregariously chanted in harmony, "And with you." Then all in sync, "Amen."

Even though we'd only known each other less than a year, Elizabeth, a dear friend, chanted even louder, "AMEN!" Exiting the church hall, we smiled and hugged briefly, feeling rejoiced after hearing the preacher's uplifting sermon.

Inhaling the fresh crisp air, we began our five block sunny day stroll. The anticipation of having brunch at our favorite French-American Bistro almost warranted a jog, the delicate "Eggs Florentine" dish invoking excessive salivation. The weather was slightly windy and warm, without a speck of humidity. The air smelled of a honey-suckle and lilac blend, the birds were chirping as if trying to say, "Oh spectacular San Francisco Bay Area day."

Ah! July, a spectacular summer month in the Menlo Park area. In Chicago or Virginia, the prior living locations for Elizabeth and me, it would've been too darned hot to venture outside for a five-block stroll. Hazy wavering heat waves rose from the concrete, typical in July for the eastern and midwest regions of the United States. Sweat, that salty tasting, wet byproduct of systemic body waste, streamed down our faces as if we were running on a treadmill at a speed of 7.0 miles per hour.

Suddenly, like a quick flash of lightning in the sky, two of the biggest black crows I have ever seen flew up and cruised over our heads. Their raucous calls pierced the air with an explosive screech, as if they were pissed off about something, or trying to urgently capture our attention. Startled, I looked up, pointed, and turned to Elizabeth, angrily protesting, "The birds stopped their melancholy chirping and those two annoying crows have scared them away."

Elizabeth directly stared up at the crows while shielding her eyes from the sun with the church announcement she had clutched in her right hand. In a lower than normal tone she stated, "Maybe the birds are taking a break, resting or possibly just flew away." I shrugged my shoulders.

After walking about two blocks, I glanced up and saw the two crows were apparently keeping pace with our steps and peering down at us with those beady, coal-colored eyes, continuing to screech. I started to feel chilly despite the crisp spring day, goose bumps forming and raising the hair on my arms. Abruptly, I nervously turned to Elizabeth and quietly confessed in a whispered, hush-like tone, as if the crows could hear me, "Guess what? I have a taboo, I'm spooked of crows. I believe they represent something bad is going to happen to whomever sees and hears them." A mythical omen implies that seeing a crow might signal an upcoming death or a catastrophic event.

Elizabeth, my dear Bohemian friend and a flower child of the 70's, or as now commonly referred to as a "Baby Boomer," bewilderedly stated, "No, my Doll, you're highly mistaken, crows are a sign of love! I read that two crows are like white doves, signaling that a couple will fall in love."

I would have expected this analogy from her, since she was again infatuated with her high school sweetheart. They had met twenty years ago and recently reunited at a high school reunion, just like in that old song, "Reunited."

The problem with this "old flame" was that he was married, promising Elizabeth he would get a divorce. Surprisingly, she was willing to wait. I kept telling Elizabeth, "Please, don't hold your breath, this is a recipe for disaster." I hated to be so blunt, but Elizabeth was paying a psychic big bucks for guidance, and I wished she could see that she was going to end up broke... and alone.

Once we finally reached our destination at the restaurant, the crows let out one final piercing loud screech and then, as abruptly they came, they flew away as if summoned by a commanding presence, possibly a whisper from a ghost.

The incident stayed on my mind the rest of the day, week, month and even years.

One

Mayaline

It's ironic how an innocent leisurely day activity, parking the car on the rocky gravel paved road by the San Mateo Bridge to watch airplanes start the smooth descent for landing at the San Francisco airport, would have such an effect one's life... my life.

Multicultural folks seeking fresh air or adrenaline junkies in overdrive looked so elated, walking or jogging the path along the shore. The hustle and bustle of everyday life in the twenty-first century rarely permits leisure time to casually enjoy a relaxing day.

I glanced up to the sky like a small child glaring in the face a parent, either pleading for attention or displeased about an occurrence. I stared in awe at the airplanes swooping slowly and precisely above an orange, blue and grey pillow pocket of clouds, setting a course across the choppy waters to land on the runway that starts in the bay at SFO airport. I sighed as my thoughts erratically wandered between my id and ego, searching, and managed a gleeful smile, and then I whimpered sadly, wiping the tears from my weary, dark-circled, deep-seated eyes. After a few minutes I smiled again, closed my eyes, put my hand up to my heart and thought of her... Mayaline.

Perky Mayaline was terrified of flying. Despite this fear, she was in awe of airplanes. The American Airline craft was her favorite plane. She loved the red, white and blue colors, just like the flag of the United States. "I'm proud to be an American, she would say, "We have the patriotic airplanes."

Considering Mayaline's infatuation with this aircraft, I made an effort to book and fly the majority of my business flights with American Airlines. On each flight, I made it a point to call her. Once I settled in my seat before that parallel pull in the air, she would ask, "Are you flying American?" Smiling to myself, I would proudly admit "Yes!" Then I'd hear a giggle, full of delight and admiration.

"Okay, my biggest flying advocate, I have to hang up. The flight attendant is cracking the whip for the cell phone turn off. I'll call you when I land."

She would answer with concern, "Make sure you do, I'm going to be worried to death."

"Please don't fret, all will be fine, remember I'm flying your favorite aircraft... American."

After hearing her ingenuous sigh, I smiled, shut off my phone and closed my eyes as the plane took off on the runway and then the classic parallel pull up, up and away into the clouds.

Since I had a hectic schedule working in a sales position for a Fortune 500 corporation with no time for family or friends, a few months had passed and I suddenly remembered that I had to buzz Mayaline to announce a sudden, life-changing decision.

Today would be a sensational day.

I dialed Mayaline and abruptly blurted, "I have a surprise, Mayaline."

"What... what is it?" she eagerly asked.

"I'm getting married in two months and I want you to attend the wedding."

"Wow, marriage? You, my dear non-domesticated prima donna?" This is shocking to me!

"Why not me," I asked?

No reply, just silence for a few minutes.

She went on to ask, "Who's the unlucky fella?" Then she quickly smirked, "I'm just kidding." She knew about my mate, Jean Paul.

"Um, the only practical way to reach you is by plane... right?"

"Right, what a treat for you since you'll be flying American I teased."

"Yippee for me"... she hastily barked with a bit of apprehension. Mayaline's daunting fear of flying wouldn't permit her to miss this festive, joyous celebration.

The eve of the wedding came as fast as a bolt of lightning in a storm.

To my relief, *Mayaline's first flight* was without incident, though she was mentally exhausted from the fear of flying when I picked her up at the airport.

I was proud of Mayaline being so daring and a brave heart, besides being loving and caring about me.

I had chosen to have my bridesmaid wear red and I wore a cream satin dress, similar to the colors of American Airlines. I had planned a patriotic color theme to show my deepest adoration and heartfelt appreciation to Mayaline for flying from coast to coast to attend my wedding... a true trooper.

"Oh... happy day," back up singers. "Oh... happy day, when Jesus walked," Humming this song made me think of the happiest day in a bride's life; love and happiness is what girls think about... marital bliss.

Unfortunately, matrimony can turn out to be a disastrous experience. A horrific verbal fight erupted between me and Jean Paul, my French groom. Mayaline witnessed this torrid argument and she looked mortified and in shock.

Extremely embarrassed, and angered beyond reason, I turned on my heels and let out a huge scream, stormed out the front door and stood in the driveway in the humid, smoldering hot Modesto sun.

After composing myself, I walked back in the house past Jean Paul and, without uttering a word, grabbed Mayaline by the hand and pulled her into the bedroom. Secretly, in a low whisper, I confessed that I never loved Jean Paul. He was a condescending, stupid, asshole bastard.

She said, "Bird, you don't have to continue with the wedding." This was her nickname for me when she wanted to soothe my discomfort and make a disturbing episode peaceful.

Regretful feelings and thoughts, about letting everyone down and all the money spent began to eat at my conscience and rattle my nerves. Then that famous guilty slogan rolled off my tongue, "I'll look like a fool and be talked about amongst my family and friends."

Mayaline firmly said, "You can work on those problems later."

Despite her words of wisdom, I decided to go ahead and take the marriage vows. What Mayaline didn't know was that Jean Paul and I had been feverishly fighting on and off for a year. Clearly we were not marriage material, but I had just turned thirty and was feeling desperate. Another grandiose problem, I was pregnant, two weeks along. I didn't want to tell anyone yet, not even my best friend who was my bridesmaid or Mayaline. This was partly due to shame. I always felt a girl should be married before she got pregnant. I had this white picket fence mentality. If I'd known then what I know today, twenty years later, those thoughts would have been a fleeting mirage of common sense.

"Regrets," that gut wrenching learned lesson. The marriage ended in divorce three months later. Jean Paul and I had gotten in a huge fight a week after the wedding. He was mad that I was eating food from a burger joint and I didn't cook dinner. He grabbed the food, threw it on me, and then kicked me in my stomach. I threw up, and a few days later had an abortion. I couldn't fathom the thought of having a baby by this animal, the dreadful thought of having to deal with him the rest of my life petrified me.

It was for the best.

I sold the newly built, four bedroom house at a loss and paid for the difference with a loan from my modest savings; I didn't want the bad credit from a foreclosure. The only precious keepsake I kept from the wedding was a picture of Mayaline with a beaming smile. I had a burning party for the photo's of the groom. It felt so wonderful, like a cleansing of the mind, body and soul.

I never married again.

Mayaline's second flight was to save her life.

For some bizarre reason, I had slept restlessly and dreamed that I was drowning in the ocean, I didn't know how to swim and was not sure why I was in water. I was sinking to the bottom with a stingray waiting to engulf me. No one was in sight to save me.

I quickly awoke and noticed that my whole body was trembling, much like a seizure, but I couldn't come out of the tremor. After about five minutes, I jolted upright in bed. I've always had a horrible fear of water. Since the age of eighteen, I'd had the same recurring dream. I never figured out what was the true meaning of the dream. In reality, I didn't want to know. I was horrified and just wanted to forget. Feeling overwhelmed and tired, I sank my head into my pillow and fell into a deep sleep.

I awoke to the phone ringing. It was Mayaline's sister calling to let me know that Mayaline was in the hospital.

"I'm at the hospital and they are running tests on Mayaline. It might not be good, according to her physician."

Still groggy, I asked, "What is the problem?" "Why isn't Mayaline calling me to deliver the news?" Having previously worked as a nurse, I was accustomed to acting calm in the presence of pending bad news related to a health concern. Nevertheless, I forcefully blurted, "Let me talk to Mayaline."

"Hello, what do you want?" she said in a defiant tone.

"Barbara called to inform me of your hospitalization."

"What do you care?" Mayaline and I had a bad tortuous, evil tongued argument the week prior, so I was the last person on her mind.

I remember being so blindsided with anger that, without thinking, I had shouted, "Just die." I had never in my life talked so harshly to Mayaline. Now she started to cry and I apologized for the hurtful words. People say things when they are angry to hurt others, such a vicious cycle of protecting one's feelings or self esteem.

"Well, I care a lot."

Mayaline then added, "I'll tell you the final test results once they're back."

Mayaline never wanted anyone to worry about her. She'd been accustomed to taking care of herself since the age of twelve, a real trooper and matriarch despite all obstacles.

She handed the phone back to Barbara.

"We'll keep you posted," Barbara whispered.

"I'll be so worried until I hear back from you guys, so please do."

Blue, Barbara's brother, called next and shared, "Maya-line used to call me screaming in pain, from her back."

"Dammit," I yelled, "Why didn't you call and tell me? Everyone is so dysfunctional and secretive. You say something at this juncture? How long has this been going on?"

"For the past six years," Blue stated. "She'd call me crying uncontrollably." In a sorrowful tone, he spewed,"I thought you knew."

The next day, that dreaded call came with the results that Mayaline was fatally ill.

I remained calm and immediately kicked into action after Barbara announced the results from the tests. Adrenaline running like a rushing river through my body. I called one of the premier hospitals in the Bay Area and spoke to the admissions coordinator for the patient intake records. Mayaline's case was accepted one week later and she was to report to the clinic the next Monday.

I called her to pack her bags and get on the next flight out of Chicago into San Francisco.

Two

The City by the Bay

Mayaline arrived at San Francisco airport, and I waited for her by the curb at the arrival area. I heard a soft tap on the window of my BMW 525 and I turned to see a beautiful, delicate sight... Mayaline her youthful, pristine face stared in at me through the passenger window.

I was upbeat as I opened the passenger door and shouted, "Hi Dee Dee," This was Mayaline's nickname. Anyone who called her this over the years, was guaranteed a warm, loving response. Not this time.

"Hi," she said sadly. "I just want you know I'm only here, because of you. I wanted to stay at the hospital in Chicago and get treated at home."

"I know, but this is the best hospital in the nation and after your medical file was reviewed, the physician was optimistic. This can be cured. Can't get any better than that," I added. "At least, you'll be skipping the horrid winter in Chicago." I tried to instill some confidence and cheer.

I was a die hard bachelorette, so I only had a cheaply framed futon and a treadmill in my spare room. This is where Mayaline slept until we arrived at the clinic the following Monday.

Mayaline wasn't too happy, because she'd worn makeup at my request. She'd protested, "We're not going to a dance, I'm going to get my life saved. I never wear makeup."

"We have to look presentable." I don't know what I was thinking. I suspect I was trying to be optimistic and thought that wearing makeup to a physician consultation would be a positive act of courage.

I was a basket case, trying to contend with difficulties and hold it all together without screeching and yelling at God.

The physician offered hope in her assessment, I was so elated to see Mayaline smile when the doctor announced, "This condition can be cured, but with no absolute guarantee." "We'll do all we can," she added.

The physician team scheduled the first outpatient treatment in December. Thanksgiving was two weeks away, so December sounded like a foreign word.

Mayaline's third flight.

It had been one week since the first clinic date, but it felt like a year. Mayaline wasn't happy about the wait period for treatment. She was mad and kept saying,"If I was in Chicago, the treatment would have started long ago."

Emotionally exhausted, Mayaline fell into a deep sleep on my futon after taking her pain medication for her back. I decided to get some rest as well.

Loudly, with an irritated tone, I heard my name called early the next morning. I bolted up in bed, looked at the clock and it was 5:00 a.m. It was Mayaline calling me. My bedroom is downstairs, so I leaped up the steps, two at a time, thinking something was wrong. There was Mayaline, sitting on the steps leading out the door with her coat on and purse on her shoulder.

I asked, "Why are you dressed in a coat this time of the morning?"

"I'm leaving," she said

"Going where?" We are scheduled to report to the clinic in about three weeks to begin the outpatient treatment.

No comment, she just kept quiet with her head down.

"I'm going back downstairs to sleep, it's so early."

I awoke for work at 7:30 a.m. and immediately rushed upstairs to make coffee. As I reached the top of the steps, I was pleased to see that Mayaline was not sitting on the steps. I rushed to the back room of the house to peer in on Mayaline to see if she was still sleep. I opened the spare bedroom, and no Mayaline. She was gone.

I immediately thought, maybe she went to McDonald's, her favorite breakfast place in the world. I called her cell and no answer. I called again in fifteen minutes. No answer. Dammit, where could she be I asked myself?

I then called Chicago to see if anyone had heard from Mayaline; the answer from the dysfunctional troops was "nada."

I decided to get in my car and drive to McDonald's, thinking she was sitting in there and having breakfast. It was only four blocks from my house. No sight of Mayaline eating amongst the hungry breakfast eaters.

I thought to myself. She'll call me in a bit, so I went back home to get dressed for work. Since I worked from home, I set my own hours, so today would result in a late start day.

12 noon, no word from Mayaline. She never answered her cell through out the day.

I couldn't file a missing report with the police, she was an adult and only seven hours had passed. I called the nearby hospitals, no Mayaline. All I could do within twenty-hour hours was sit and wait.

To my amazement, I slept peacefully through the night.

The next morning, I decided to call Mayaline home's number. She answered. She was back in Chicago.

"How could you do this to me?" I asked. I was worried sick. I was curious how she got to the airport from the East Bay to SFO, but maybe she left out of Oakland to Chicago. I didn't care at this point, I was mostly concerned with her well being.

She said, "After you went mad and acted like a crazy woman the other day, screaming and yelling, slamming chairs in the living room and acting like a deranged, crazy woman, I decided to leave."

I remember the incident vividly. I was stressed about everything that had happened. I didn't like seeing Mayaline unhappy and this just sent me spiraling into a stress fit. She didn't want to celebrate Thanksgiving and I tried hard to keep a festive environment.

"I'm so sorry," I added, I can imagine how you feel. Please, please come back. I don't want you in Chicago all alone."

"No," protested Mayaline, "I'm checking myself into the hospital tomorrow to begin treatment. I don't want to be in California."

"Please," I begged. "You'll get the best treatment at the academic hospital I chose. They specialize in the condition. They are known to cure patients, and I worked at that hospital for three years."

"I'm very tired and I need to go lie down," stated Mayaline.

"OK," I added." Have a great night's rest and I'll call you in the morning."

Early the next morning I called Mayaline, still begging and pleading for her to come back. Finally, she decided to come back to California.

Mayaline's fourth flight.

She arrived two days later. I was glad and relieved to see her, but I don't think the feeling was mutual. Mayaline looked disgusted, drained and tired. Gracefully, I settled her back in my home, while I walked on eggshells to ensure that everything went smoothly without havoc-ridden situations.

Mayaline wasn't eating well. Her appetite had succumbed to worry and despair. I felt helpless and tried hard to coax her into the holiday spirits, mainly Thanksgiving. This holiday was not a priority for her happiness, only starting her treatment. We still had two weeks to go.

Another work day rolled around. I was downstairs in my bedroom getting ready for work and I heard a chilling, shrieking scream from upstairs. Frantically, I ran upstairs and found Mayaline standing up in the bathtub, naked, crying and shaking. Shrieking loudly in fear, Mayaline yelled "My legs are numb and I know something is terribly wrong. Please, let's go to the hospital."

As a nurse, I thought maybe this was a fleeting symptom of the disease and possibly nothing too serious. I tried to calm Mayaline and said, "Don't worry, it'll probably subside in a few hours, let's watch it. We're due at the clinic in nine days."

"Please, PLEASE take me to the hospital!" Mayaline screamed." This is something else. Oh, please, help me!. She continued to scream, crying uncontrollably. "We have to go to the hospital... now!"

I spewed exhaustedly, "We'll go when I get home from work." I hurried back downstairs to jump in the shower and get dressed.

As I stepped in the shower, I heard the front door slam. I exited the shower, wet and sprung back upstairs.

Mayaline was gone.

I sprinted naked into the garage, grabbed a coat and jumped into my car. I slammed the gas pedal and backed the car out of the garage.

As I looked up and down the street, I couldn't see Mayaline, so I decided to turn right at the next corner. I could see Mayaline walking, so I pulled alongside her and begged her to get in the car, so that I could take her to the hospital. She was enraged and refused. I tried again and the answer was still, "No, just go away, go to work and leave me alone"

I had to go back home and put on some clothes, I was naked under my coat, so I turned around and went back home to throw on some clothes.

Fifteen minutes later, I drove fast in the same direction Mayaline was walking, but there was no sight of her. I called her cell, no answer.

I decided to drive to the nearest hospital and there I found Mayaline sitting in the ER waiting room. I asked how she got there and she stated, "I flagged down an ambulance and they brought me here."

Mayaline was admitted and I made sure she was settled in bed. I felt a big relief, knowing that they would run tests and find out what was wrong. The hospital ran tests, just not the needed MRI, even after two additional admissions for leg weakness. She was put on a nerve pain medicine and I rubbed her legs with Ben Gay at night. These measures helped some, but I was counting down the days until December 10.

Mayaline was still able to walk, but with moderate weakness. I went to the local drugstore and bought Mayaline a cane. One evening while Mayaline was standing at the kitchen sink, I heard a loud thump. She had fallen and I found her sitting on her butt in her pajamas. I gently lifted her up and helped her onto the couch. I was pleased that she drifted off into a peaceful sleep.

While she slept, all I could think of was to go and grab the Ben Gay and rub it on her lower legs and feet, plus elevate them on pillows. I felt so terribly bewildered and scared.

Three

Praise the Day

Monday, December 10, finally came. I had to get a wheelchair to take Mayaline into the clinic from the car. By this time, Mayaline's leg movement was severely impaired and weak, despite the medications she had been taking for the condition prescribed at the local hospital. The leg weakness had worsened to a point of ataxia when she walked for even a brief distance.

The clinic nurse practitioner became furious. With heightened irritability and a distorted face, she turned to me and yelled, "She wasn't like this when we saw her a month ago! Why didn't you bring her back to be checked out for this new condition?" With pin-pointed pupils, she glared at me and snarled, "Just wait until the attending physician finds this out."

Startled, I stepped back a few steps and stared at the nurse as if she was an alien. Overcome with apprehension, I cried in protest, "I thought the local hospital in my neighborhood could treat the leg weakness." This was the lowest I had felt since this whole illness had inflicted Mayaline. I told myself, she's in good hands and they'll get her better at this cutting-edge, ivy league hospital.

Mayaline was rushed down the clinic hall to the emergency room to be admitted to the hospital. Immediately after the admission, she was started on her first dose of chemotherapy that evening, and radiation was to begin the following week.

As I walked next to Mayaline on the gurney to her first radiation treatment, I smelled the putrid odor of burning flesh in the radiation treatment center. I was hoping that Mayaline didn't smell this odor. If she did, she kept quiet. No matter how the hospital cleaned with disinfectants, a nurse can pick up on that distinct flesh smell.

Two weeks later, I entered Mayaline's hospital room to feed her breakfast. As I strolled to the bedside to fix her tray, she blurted in excitement, "Bird," my nickname given to me by Mayaline, "I think I can move my legs a little." Then she grabbed my arm and gave me a pinch. I smiled a big grin, because if Mayaline called me "Bird" and pinched me, she was in good spirits.

I delightfully replied, "Let me, let me see." I then touched her legs to feel the movement and I could feel the wiggle in her toes. We both were overcome with joy! "Now hope is our new friend," we sang as we hugged each other and I planted a kiss on her forehead."

Three weeks had passed and Mayaline continued to receive the chemotherapy and radiation treatments. I started to see clearly (as the song goes) with belief that Mayaline was in good care and receiving the treatment that would cure her. In no time, she would return home to Chicago.

With my spirits being lifted, I decided to dabble at dating. I hadn't been in a relationship for two years. With the stress of my new employment and Mayaline getting sick, I felt that I needed some me time. I answered a singles ad on a popular singles site and began communicating with a man from a neighboring city. We decided to meet at a local coffee shop near my house.

I had informed him that it would have to be a late coffee date since I would return from the hospital fairly late. Unfortunately, I was quite a bit late. As I walked into the coffee shop, at first I didn't see anyone else in the facility. Then I spotted a dark, olive-skinned guy sitting at a corner table in the back. I approached this man and asked was he the guy from the singles dating site, and he stated, "Yes," and he smiled.

To my ultimate horror, his smile resembled the teeth of a prehistoric dinosaur, and then he didn't look human.

Scared out of my wits, all I could say was, "Why do you have so many teeth?"

19

In a raspy voice, he responded that he was born this way.

I shot back with, "I'm surprised you haven't seen a dentist to repair your teeth; dentures would suit you well." He didn't respond to my statement.

A wave of fear overcame my body, and I felt like bolting out of the coffee shop. I had never in my life seen anyone's mouth look blatantly hideous and distorted. As a nurse, I had witnessed some unsettling sights in my career, but this visual picture top anything abnormal I've ever seen. As an added horrific bonus, his voice was unusual and strange.

For some crazy reason I sat down thinking, "He can't help that he looks like a monster when he smiled." After conversing with this man for about thirty minutes, I had to leave! I couldn't tolerate the grizzly sight of his teeth and it appeared that his mouth stretched to compensate for the massive number of teeth. The teeth didn't even look like human teeth; they were long, fanged teeth crowded on top of each other with a dark brownish color to all of them. He looked like the Devil from Hell, a demon.

I hurriedly stood up, yelled "Goodbye," excused myself, rushed to the door, and then sprinted to my car that was parked in front of the coffee shop.

When I arrived home, all I could think about was what or who did I just meet? Was this a creature from hell? An omen? We never communicated again, and I never dated another person from this singles site.

A menacing common hospital problem occurred. Mayaline contracted a urinary tract infection from the indwelling foley catheter in her bladder. The timing couldn't have been worse. She was to be discharged to a rehabilitation center to strengthen her lower extremities per the treating physician team.

Mayaline only lasted a week in the rehabilitation hospital. She had to call 911 one night from her hospital bed. She was having chest pain and turned on her call light, but no nurse came to the room. They were having a Christmas holiday celebration.

The ambulance came and took Mayaline back to the hospital. She was admitted again. It was discovered that her urinary tract infection had severely worsened, despite her being sent out on a prescription course of a "standard of care" broad-spectrum oral antibiotic. Within the next few days, she began to have copious amount of blood in her urinary collection bag, signaling that she was bleeding from her bladder. It was evident that the first antibiotic she was put on was the wrong choice and this agent didn't clear the infection, it evidently made it spiral out of control.

The next morning when I entered the hospital room to feed Mayaline, I noted that she was quieter than usual and had a sad look on her face, so I asked, "Is anything wrong?"

She replied, "Yes, the ambulance paramedic was mean to me. He kept sticking me with the intravenous catheter, trying to start an IV line in my vein. I kept telling him that I had bad veins, but he screamed at me and harshly told me to shut up. I started to cry hysterically and this made him even more irate at me."

I became furious and immediately called the ambulance company and reported the incident. I tried to soothe Mayaline by stating that some folks take their job too seriously and that can cause harm to others. In sorrow, I apologized that I wasn't there to accompany her to the hospital. In this instance, I just think the ambulance paramedic was just cruel, probably hated his job, working nights.

After I hung up the phone, I informed Mayaline that I had taken took care of the unfortunate incident and hopefully the creep will be fired.

After Mayaline had been in the hospital for three weeks, her urine turned clear and the case manager warden was licking her lips again. This time Mayaline was discharged to another rehabilitation facility. I had chosen a facility three miles up the street from the hospital. The building looked great on the outside and the lobby was well manicured, but once you entered the resident floors on the top levels, the units looked like an old psychiatric ward. The beds looked like they had been in the rooms since the 1900s. The food was bland and tasteless.

Mayaline couldn't eat anything that was served to her, so I prepared her meals, even though I wasn't a great cook. I thought, we won't be here long. Mayaline will walk out of here after her physical therapy. Twice a week, "She would be transported to the treating hospital in an ambulance for her chemotherapy and radiation treatment."

The continued outpatient oncology appointments resulted in Mayaline losing sixty pounds and she suffered severe dehydration. She couldn't eat due to the sores in her mouth and throat from the radiation. She also suffered burnt skin from the radiation. I would rub soothing cocoa butter and Aloe Vera gel on her skin and bring in soft food for her throat. Mashed potatoes and gravy, her favorite, plus vanilla-flavored milk shakes.

The physical therapy sessions didn't render any positive outcomes. Mayaline had a thoracic surgery consult and the tumor had spread, pressing on her spine. The surgeon stated that she wasn't a good candidate for surgery, so we had to be at the mercy of God, the chemotherapy and radiation to shrink the diseased tissue.

As time moved slowly, like a snail creeping in the Bay Area fog, I'd frequently witness Mayaline crying, pounding her head on the bed rails, in pure turmoil and desperation over trying to walk again. I was praying that she'd regain her strength and movement in her lower extremities. She was continually getting weaker. Her skin turgor presented severe signs of dehydration.

I called the charge nurse one afternoon and demanded that Mayaline be started on intravenous saline or D5W fluids to rehydrate her. She wasn't a diabetic. As a result of my persistence, thankfully saline was ordered by the medical director at the nursing home. To my horror, as the nurse came in to start the intravenous fluids, the head nurse commented on how beautiful Mayaline was and what a gorgeous body she had at sixty. "What an awful thing to say," I thought. This was San Francisco and one never knew if a female was a lesbian or straight. She sounded like the latter, so I just commented, "Family genes."

Mayaline had enough torture! As I walked into the room one night after work and I started to put her hospital gown on she screamed, "Please help me, Bird!"

That hit a strong chord with me, especially being a dedicated nurse to patients many years ago. I briskly hurried out of the room and asked the relief charge nurse on duty to call the hospital and have Mayaline admitted ASAP! Her condition was rapidly deteriorating.

Surprisingly, she turned to me and yelled, "You're trespassing and interfering with Mayaline's care!" Then I heard her say, "I'm calling the police."

I fiercely howled, "Call the cops and in the interim, I'm calling an ambulance to have Mayaline transferred to the emergency room."

I dialed an ambulance on my cell phone. Within fifteen minutes, the ambulance arrived with a gurney. I marched them to Mayaline's room. I hugged Mayaline and with a sigh, I smiled and said, "Mayaline we're leaving and going to the hospital." She was quiet, but I got a sense she was relieved to leave this dungeon.

As the paramedics were strapping her to the gurney, two cops appeared. They asked what was the situation at hand. I explained that Mayaline was very sick and I was taking her to the hospital since the nursing home refused to call the medical director and have her transferred. "I added, if you need to take me to jail, then it'll have to wait until Mayaline is transferred to the hospital, she needs emergent care."

The police appeared sympathetic, sorrowful and stated, "Do what is necessary and don't worry, you're not going to jail."

As the ambulance was boarding the elevator with Mayaline, I looked back and saw the maggot nurse bitch peering around the corner. When she saw me looking towards her, she darted inside the door.

"Good riddance, hell hole and sicko employees!" I shouted.

At the emergency room at her original treating hospital, Mayaline's labs were extremely abnormal. Another foley catheter was put in and the urinalysis sample showed an obvious urinary infection. The same infection she had when she first left the hospital lingered, despite treatment with three antibiotics. We were both relieved to be in the hospital safe and sound at least, so we thought.

Back on the unit floor, Mayaline was in better spirits and I was relieved to have her in the care of hospital experts and felt she would be able to go back home to Chicago soon.

I started to notice that Mayaline began to moan at night in despair. She was tired and had been through a lot, dealing with the hospitals, transfers, horrible ambulance staff and nursing homes. Physical therapy wasn't going well and her lower limbs were atrophying, revealing the tibia and fibia bones with sparse muscle, so it was even harder for her to stand without falling.

I begged her doctors to order the acute level physical therapy, so that she would receive more extensive rehabilitation in order for her to regain her normal activities of daily living. The answer was that she didn't qualify, because she had to be able to perform three normal daily activities on her own. Just another hospital bullshit policy.

Despite my recently starting a new job, I was determined to be there for Mayaline and at the same time complete my excessively demanding employment duties.

My systematic ritual: alarm goes off at 4:00 a.m., time to get up and get to the hospital an hour away to feed and bathe Mayaline, and then off to work from the hospital and back in the evening for the nighttime ritual.

As I entered the room, the nurse's aide walked in after me, assessing her assignment for the day and then she left quickly. I began to run the water for Mayaline's bed bath. As I checked her diaper, I noticed that her diaper was saturated with urine. I immediately began to bathe her, to rid her body of the urine smell. I couldn't quite turn her on her side by myself, so I pushed the call bell on to ask the nurse's aide for help in turning Mayaline to wash her tush.

The nurse's aide stormed in the room and asked what I needed. After telling her I needed help to bathe and turn Mayaline, she yelled, "I have a ten-patient assignment and I don't have time to help you." I protested and stated that I was doing her a favor by bathing Mayaline, so she should at least help.

She finally helped me turn Mayaline on her side, so that I could give her tush a good wash from the urine smell. As I was drying her bottom, I patted her buttock cheeks and stated, "Mayaline you're all clean."

A few minutes later, a familiar face entered the room... Mayaline's social worker. She asked me to step out of the room. I asked what was the problem and she stated there's a complaint that I hit Mayaline. I was aghast and I immediately blurted, "You are kidding... right?"

"No," she stated in a matter-of-fact tone. "In this instance, we'll have to file a battery report with the state department and in the interim, you are not allowed to enter Mayaline's room without supervision, plus you'll have a time limit of an hour."

I tried to explain that the nurse's aide was in a sour mood this morning and was obviously, trying to seek revenge. In desperation, I explained the bathing incident where I patted Mayaline on her buttocks as a gesture that we were done.

The social worker wasn't buying any part my story, so I stormed away and ran to my car in the parking lot. I had to get home to hire an attorney. The staff at the hospital didn't like me because I'm a Registered Nurse who they knew would fight for quality care for Mayaline. I worked at the hospital back in the 80's and cared for hundreds of patients without incident. What a direct attack on my professional integrity and professionalism!

I made it home, contacted the nearest criminal defense attorney that I could find, three blocks from my house. I explained the situation to counsel Lowkowski. He decided to take the case, but asked for a one thousand dollar retainer, which I eagerly paid. Mr. Lowkowski promised he would immediately contact the social worker to get the ball rolling and have the hospital or social agency dismiss the ludicrous charge against me.

I went back to the hospital to see Mayaline. As I entered the room, the nurse was on my heels, stating that I had to check in at the nursing station each time I visited Mayaline, and I was only permitted an hour visit. I then hurried to the social worker's office. She was sitting at her desk. I peeked my head in the door and informed her that I hired an attorney and that he would be in touch with her. She stated, "I already have a message from him, but in the interim, you're to follow our orders. I walked away in total disgust, entered Mayaline's room and sat quietly by her. She was sleeping.

Unfortunately, hiring the attorney turned out to be a wild goose chase. He explained that the hospital never returned his calls and if I wanted him to continue working on the case, I would have to pay another thousand dollars. I didn't have the money, so I opted for defeat. Despite the outcome, I was proud that I fought the absurd allegations.

After this blatant act against me, I decided to get Mayaline out of California and transfer her to a hospital in the South, her home state, Mississippi. I thought, maybe this hospital staff would be more caring and supportive. I called over six facilities in the Mississippi area, only to be denied transfer acceptance based on the Medicare transfer policy. Mayaline's acuity level and diagnosis placed her in a high risk status.

I decided to go without the transfer approval from the receiving facilities in Mississippi. I figured that if we just showed up at the emergency room, they would have to admit her.

I informed the treating physicians of my plans and there was nothing they could do to stop me. They threatened that they couldn't sign for the transfer, so it would be deemed against medical advice to relocate to another facility.

I made the flight arrangements, paid for three tickets for me, Mayaline and a close friend who would help with her care in flight. I called the airline and arranged for a wheelchair and oxygen were confirmed.

Two days before we were to fly, Mayaline became sick with a critical respiratory infection and her oxygen saturation wouldn't progress pass 80 percent. The physicians warned that with her lung condition, if Mayaline went up in the air at a high altitude she could die.

Therefore, I cancelled the plans. I had to tell Mayaline that we couldn't go, and she was devastated. I assured her that once she got a little stronger and more stable, we'd leave for the South. She nodded her head, "Okay." The tickets would be good for a year, so I was optimistic based on this promise.

After one week, the case manager warden lashed her exit whip: back to the nursing home. They called it rehabilitation strengthening. I was appalled that the hospital would send a patient who was not stable out to a nursing homes. I later found out that the reasoning for this act of hurriedness was based on Medicare inpatient to outpatient standards of care, commonly referred to as the CMS rule.

Mayaline ended up at a facility on the other side of Bay, across the mildly choppy waters of the San Mateo Bridge. I decided this would be more optimal and easier for me to get to Mayaline, since I lived in the East Bay. As usual, the nursing homes was dreadful looking, with a putrid smell of urine and feces. Maybe it was due to the older building or the care of the patients. At this point, I wished that I had better managed my finances to have an adequate reserve for desperate times like now. The slogan, "Save for a rainy day" sure has merit. How I dreamed of being able to place Mayaline in a five-star Cadillac facility. Unfortunately, this was not the case based on my excessive spending.

Mayaline only lasted two days at this facility. She suffered another severe respiratory distress episode. As a result of her diminished lung capacity, if she stood up, her oxygen saturation would plummet to 70 percent, putting her in a severe hypoxic state. She was too ill to be in the facility. It was so heart wrenching to see her fighting so hard for her life, only to have her body dictate another scenario.

Back to the hospital we go.

Mayaline was admitted to the nearest community hospital facility up the street from the resident care home. This time her sister came to visit from across the country on Amtrak.

A few hours after Mayaline was admitted, the social worker at this hospital visited to question the physical abuse complaint at the mothership facility. Surprised and disappointed, I became enraged over the incident. I told him my side of the story and stated I didn't want to revisit this lie again and that if this situation persisted, I would hire an attorney to protect my interests against the alleged allegations. He was a bit more warm hearted and just stated, "Okay, I'm just doing my job."

"Doing a good job has a place and time based on this urgent medical situation. A past hospital's lies should not take precedence, the patient's life is on the line," I voiced in absolute distaste for his lack of professionalism.

In the hospital, the favorable outcome was that Mayaline's spirits lifted when her sister entered her room and stayed by her bedside for a few days.

The hospital physical therapists worked diligently with Mayaline, but she still couldn't stand or have enough strength to endure the sessions. I thought about hiring a personal trainer to come in and strengthen her atrophied lower extremities, but I needed a doctor's order as this would be seen as interference with care.

Since Mayaline's appetite improved a bit, she became a tad bit stronger. Three weeks had passed and the bedsore had grown to the size of a quarter, but the area continued to be superficial with no depth to the wound.

She remained incontinent of stool in her diaper; the foley catheter was in, collecting her urine. A dark amber color signaled that Mayaline wasn't drinking enough water and needed fluids. She continued on multiple courses of IV antibiotics for treatment of her urinary tract infection. For some daunting, unexplainable reason, the urinary infection lingered and would not clear with the choice of agents selected by the various physician practitioners. She was in and out of confusion, but the majority of the days she was alert. I was so pleased that her sister was present.

To my distaste, the case manager entered the room for the discharge papers to be signed for discharge to another nursing home. I refused, stating that Mayaline's next discharge should be to go home, not back to those facilities that never do any good for her care. I stated that based on her confusion, she couldn't legally sign the documents to have herself transferred to another facility. To my amazement, they arranged for a psychiatry consult and he ruled she was coherent. I refuted the documentation and told the team that the psychiatrist conducted the meeting without my presence, plus she was possibly coached into saying what the psychiatrist needed to satisfy the hospital's requirements to have her discharged. Since this was a legal HIPPAA protected document, I couldn't do anything to have it changed or have the consult redone with a family member present. At least, not to my knowledge.

I walked into Mayaline's room the next day and she was crying, yelling and protesting that she had to go the post office to get her social security check to pay her rent or she'd be evicted, she thought she was in Chicago. I felt so sorry for Mayaline. All she wanted was to be well and be back in Chicago, not transferred to another nursing home.

The most devastating blow was when her sister announced that she had to leave. I begged her stay, because Mayaline would need her at this new nursing home. As far as I know, she didn't have any reason to go home. She was single, not employed, and kids grown.

After everything that Mayaline had endured, the worst

blow to her spirits and confidence was when her sister turned to leave. Mayaline reached her arms out reach out to her sister and wailed, "Mildred, please don't go." Her sister kept walking, never turning around to acknowledge Mayaline's plea. Witnessing the whole scene, my heart felt as if I was about to have a serious myocardial infarction.

I'll never forget, nor will I ever forgive Mildred for this treacherous, insensitive act.

Now Mayaline had no one, except for me. None of her five living brothers and sisters were present to comfort her, but she had been there for their serious illnesses that almost resulted in death, and she was at the bedside of the other three who died.

The day came for her to be discharged back to the nursing home. I refused to sign for the transfer documents but they continued the discharge process anyway. I decided to walk out of the hospital as Mayaline was being put on the ambulance gurney. I thought by making this daring move, they would keep Mayaline and continue the acute care that she desperately needed as a result of her fragile condition.

Well, my ploy didn't work. I called the nursing home across the street from the hospital thirty minutes later, Mayaline was there, so I hurried to the facility to be with her.

While reading Mayaline's hospital records, I found out that her blood pressure had shot up to 160/100, probably due to the anxiety from being transferred again. She was distressed by witnessing me fighting so hard with the clinical staff. The team had called a code blue, but fortunately this did not result in a fatality, since her blood pressure stabilized to 130/70.

She was in a room with three other patients. It was clearly obvious that she was the youngest of the four residents. My head started to ache as I was desperately trying to think of a logical solution to getting Mayaline out of here and taking care of her at my home. I was a competent nurse, and having cared for so many patients in the past, there should be no reason for me not to care for Mayaline. Realistically though, if something happened to Mayaline at my house, like her unthinkable death, I would be guilt-ridden for the rest of my life.

Mayaline lasted one week in this desolate facility before she was back in the emergency room at the hospital across the street. I received a call at midnight from the charge nurse on the night shift. Mayaline had been transferred to the hospital because of increased agitation and confusion.

The hospital prescribed Ativan and Ritalin to treat the anxiety and then sent her back to the nursing home in an ambulance. They didn't attempt to admit her for a 24-four observation; the hospital was trying to keep her away based on the strict Medicare guidelines for recent readmission criteria.

The next morning I entered Mayaline's room and I heard her talking gregariously to Joy. Joy was her dead sister. I overheard Mayaline ask, "Joy, where are you going with that cigarette?"

Startled, I told Mayaline that Joy was not in the room.

She opened her eyes, closed them slowly and said, "Joy, is standing right there, smoking her cigarette." Then she became quiet and so did I. Shortly thereafter, she fell asleep and I thought, "Was Joy really there with Mayaline?"

I turned Mayaline, put ointment on her quarter-size wound on her coccyx, bandaged the are and made sure her diaper was clean and dry.

Later on that day, it was time for physical therapy session. I always cherished the physical therapy sessions, with the belief the therapy would help Mayaline get stronger and finally go home. This particular session didn't go well. Mayaline became short of breath and almost passed out, so we had to transfer her back to the hospital again. A respiratory treatment with steroids was administered and she was sent back to the nursing home... as usual.

Mayaline ate very little for dinner, and she refused to take her medicine. I tucked her in, kissed her goodbye, and told her I'd be back after work the next day.

The next morning I awoke with an unsettling, eerie feeling, and I was perspiring profusely. Out the clear blue, I decided to drive to the nursing home to feed Mayaline breakfast, get her bathed and dressed for the day, then go back later after work and visit with her for dinner. This was quite abnormal for me as the nursing home was in the other direction, two hours from my job location.

I drove, thinking Mayaline would be surprised to see me so early in the morning, plus I'd give her a bath instead of the nursing aide team. Mayaline had always been very private, so the action of others washing her, especially her private area, was very distressing for Mayaline. She was too weak to wash herself.

As I entered her room, I noticed that Mayaline was dressed in her velvety red jump suit that I bought for her a few days ago. She had her favorite white Adidas white tennis shoes on and thick white bobby socks. She was sitting upright in bed and her eyes were closed, so I thought she was sleeping. I went over to the bed and called her name, "Good Morning, Mayaline." No answer. Gently, I shook her, no response. I noticed her skin color looked ashen, her lips crimson and she was profusely clammy.

I ran to the door and yelled for the nurse to call a code blue. They came and took her blood pressure. No reading. Then they called the ambulance. I started to cry and screamed Mayaline's name.

The ambulance paramedic team entered the room, put the blood pressure cuff on and was able to capture a faint reading. The lead paramedic thought he heard 60/30. They lifted her onto the gurney and rushed over to the emergency room. I met them there, and the emergency room team started feverishly working on Mayaline.

Once they started fluids, she came around and I sighed, showing all my pearly whites. "Hi, Mayaline. Boy, did you scare me. Everything is going to be okay."

She lifted her head and looked up at me from the emergency room bed, frowned, then laid her head back down on the pillow. I was so relieved she was alive.

Then she had a rather large bowel movement on the gurney, and I told the nurse that I would take care of the incident. The nurse yelped, "Wait, I have to send a stool specimen to the lab for testing." After the specimen was obtained, I cleaned Mayaline and put on a fresh diaper.

Afterwards, Mayaline was transferred to ICU. Before I left her bedside, the ICU physician came and informed me that her stool specimen had came back positive for serious Clostridium Difficile infection. With angst, I became frightened. The C-Diff organism can be deadly, with patients succumbing to a terrible death. I hired a certified nurse's aide sitter to watch over Mayaline while I went to work.

When I returned after work, Mayaline's condition had deteriorated. To help her breathe, she was intubated and hooked up to a respirator. The deadly organism was leading Mayaline towards a severe sepsis syndrome. The Clostridium bacteria invaded her body as a result of the resistant bacteria that continually harbored in her system from a urinary tract infection that was previously treated with the wrong antibiotics and her damaged white blood cells caused by the chemotherapy and radiation.

Later that night, she started to present with violent seizures. Mayaline was taken by way of gurney for an emergency MRI of the brain and the test was normal, which was very odd.

The physician and pharmacy team put her on a Dilantin drip to control the seizures. Her kidneys had stopped producing urine, and her body was edematous and she wasn't moving or responding to touch.

I held her hand and whispered in her ear, "Mayaline, hang in there, you can pull through this, you're strong."

Her feet started to turn blue due to the vasopressors. I hated to see her feet discolored a dark blue color and presumably cold, so as a coping mechanism, I wrapped her feet in warm blankets. I started to wash her face with a cool towel, brush her hair and rub her body down with lotion. Then I put headphones on her ears and started to play her favorite music on the tape she had in her precious Walkman tape player that I had given her as a gift last Christmas. The nurses looked at me as if I was insane.

About 1:00 a.m., I decided to go home since Mayaline was somewhat stable. I figured that she needed to rest and by tomorrow she'd come around and be herself again. As I was about to leave, the nurse stated that he didn't think she would last too much longer. "He told me her blood pressure is hovering at 60/40. Despite us titrating the vasopressors, it won't normalize."

In a stern voice, I turned to him and said, "You're not God. Only he decides how long she lasts, and she'll defeat this crisis."

The next morning at 7:00 a.m., in a complete frenzy, I got up and rushed to the hospital.

Mayaline's condition did change a bit over night. Her blood pressure was the same, fluctuating at a dangerously low reading and her respiratory status worsened. Her poor little head was being jerked back and forth as she gasped for air with the CPAP mask on her face. Mayaline was trying hard to breathe, trying to hang on to life and not succumb to death.

The doctor came and asked if I wanted to make her a "Do Not Resuscitate" and I immediately said, no. Mayaline is strong and a fighter. She would want everything medically possible down to save her life."

We'll have to remove the CPAP machine, intubate and place her on a respirator to have a chance at survival. "Ok, I agreed."

As a nurse, I knew that patients can still hear even though they are intubated and on a respirator.

The second night in ICU, now her extremities were the color of the sky at midnight. She was still seizing, eyes rolling back in her head. Her poor extremities were cool to touch. Even at that, I was still hopeful. As a nurse, I've witnessed physicians perform miracles that resulted in patient survival, even when patients bounced back from a straight line heart monitor reading, which equates to death.

To try to ease her erratic brain electrical activity, I decided to put one of my favorite CD's in her ears. I switched the CD to play the song, "I never wrote you a love song." I washed her sweaty, salty face, planted a kiss on her forehead and prayed hard and begged. 2:00 a.m. rolled around and I decided to leave to go home and catch some shut eye.

> *"Something has spoken to me in the night... and told me that I shall die, I know not where. Saying: [Death is] to lose the earth you know for greater knowing; to lose the life you have, for greater life; to leave the friends and family you loved, for greater loving; to find a land more kind than home, more larger than earth."*
>
> —THOMAS WOLFE, YOU CAN'T GO HOME AGAIN.

The next morning at 5:00 a.m. I received a call from the hospital. "Please come, Mayaline condition has turned for the worse."

Frantic, I jumped out of the bed, leaped in my car and drove the car pool lane all the way to the hospital. I wasn't supposed to be in this lane as a single driver, it was 7:30 a.m. I felt bad, but I was hell bent on getting to the hospital. To my surprise and relief, no cops stopped me during the sixty mile trip.

I ran like a deranged person into the ICU room and the Mayaline I had seen just a few hours before, had transformed into a body that was blackened with blood. Blood had oozed into her tissues, she was swollen and disfigured, and she didn't look like my Mayaline.

I was aghast! "Oh, God... no, this can't be happening." This is not the Mayaline I'd known all my life. "Jesus, Mary and Joseph please, please." I cried loudly. To see Mayaline in this condition took me back to a patient I treated when I was a young nurse at the tender age of twenty. I remember walking in the room, just I did now, and her condition was as I had just witnessed, only severely worse. The patient's tissues were filled with blood, and the blood seeped through and ran onto the floor. I was hoping the patient felt no pain, as she wasn't responsive during this systemic sequel. It was one of the worst sights I had ever experienced as a nurse, and I hoped I'd hoped never to see a patient like that again.

Now, I was witnessing Mayaline to have the same fate. Her body was blackened and swollen from the waist down. Her beautiful, amazingly radiant face was preserved for the moment.

As I looked up at the heart monitor, still hoping, her blood pressure read 50/20.

It was at this time that the ICU physician asked if I wanted a Code Blue. I stated, "Yes! Please, please save her." Other patients had come out of distressed situations, Mayaline has fought a long hard battle, she won't give up and be defeated by death.

Mayaline wasn't saved, she died.

My strong faith in the medical system and God left when Mayaline died. All I could think of at that moment was that Mayaline was just a few years from retirement and how badly she had wanted to go and live in the same retirement home with her two sisters in Chicago.

I had tried so hard to keep her dream alive by trying to have her treated at a prominent medical institution with high cure rates for cancerous patients of all types. I stayed at the bedside until the pastor arrived. He said a prayer and I asked, "Do you think she went to heaven?"

He answered, "Yes, I saw her spirit rise."

"Are you just saying this to make me feel better?"

"My blessed child," he said," I felt her spirit rise."

After he left, the nurse came to remove all the lifesaving tubes. She pulled the tape from the endotracheal tube lodged in Mayaline's throat, and to my horror, she ripped a large patch of skin from Mayaline's face. I bellowed, "Hey, HEY... You, NURSE, take it easy!"

I decided to cut a piece of Mayaline's hair to keep with me always in a special sacred angel carved box. Then I left the room and as I walked, the morgue attendant rolled by me with Mayaline on a cart draped with a brilliantly colored red cloth. I stared at the morgue cart, stricken with uncontrollably grief. I tearfully whispered, "Bye, Mayaline. I'm so sorry. Please forgive me and the healthcare system."

I walked out of the hospital doors, sat at the curb outside the hospital entrance and screamed, "Why?" Then I sobbed uncontrollably. You see, Mayaline was my beloved mom.

> *"Hundreds of dewdrops to greet the dawn,*
> *Hundreds of bees in the purple clover,*
> *Hundreds of butterflies on the lawn,*
> *But only one mother the wide world over."*

—GEORGE COOPER,"ONLY ONE MOTHER."

In speaking to the staff ICU physician, I learned that Mayaline was in a severe sepsis syndrome. The severe sepsis was caused by an emerging deadly gram negative hospital-acquired infection that was treated with numerous types and therapy courses of broad-spectrum antibiotics. C-Difficile toxin bacteria caused by excessive use of antibiotics, or as a contaminant from another patient or hospital personnel, destroyed Mayaline's gut flora and this sequence subsequently caused her body to attack itself, resulting in a complete shutdown of her organs and systemic functioning. Her immunocompromised system from the chemotherapy and radiation treatment didn't help the situation. Mayaline had no weapon against this deadly organism that can kill in 48 to 72 hours.

One year after Mayaline's death, I decided to open her precious little red bible that she kept at her bedside when she was in the hospital. I had been able to take the precious item home from the hospital the morning she died.

While flipping through the pages, I found a small piece of lined notebook paper with a message written on it in Mayaline's flawless scripted penmanship. She had written a message on it to God. She kept this secret written message between her and God buried in the pages of Psalms.

It read:

"God saw that you were getting tired and a cure was not to be. So he put his arms around you and whispered... come to thee. Lift up your hearts and peace to thee. God wanted me now."

After reading this note, tears flooded down by face, like looking out a window as a light rain would trickle down a window. The sclera in my eyes turned red as blood.

In shuffling through the additional pages, Mayaline had circled several references in the book of Psalm. The inscription that stood out was where she had inscribed her name by Psalm 23. She wrote her real name, "Ella." Psalms 23 is the scripture that soothes one's anxiety, especially in the fear of the unknown related to life or death situations.

Ella had heavily circled Psalms 22:

" My God, my God, why hast thou forsaken me. Why art thou so far from helping me, and from the words of my roaring?"

Then there was *Psalms 54*. She neatly circled verses 1 and 2.

Verse 1: "Save me, O, God, by thy name, and judge me by thy strength."

Verse 2: "Hear my prayer!" O, God, give ear to the words of my mouth."

Psalms 27, "The Lord "is" my light and my salvation, whom shall I fear?" "The Lord "is" the strength of my life; of whom shall I be afraid?"

Psalms 6: Verses 2, 3 and 4.

Verse 2: "Have mercy upon me, O, Lord; for I 'am' weak: "O, Lord, heal me, for my bones are vexed."

Verse 3: "My soul is also sore vexed: but thou, O, Lord, how long?"

Verse 4: "Return, O, Lord; deliver my soul: Oh save me for thy mercies' sake."

Psalm 55: She circled verses 4 and 6.

Verse 4: "My heart is sore and pained, and the terrors of death are fallen upon me."

Verse 6: "And I said, Oh Lord that I had wings like a dove!" For then I would fly away and be set at rest."

Mayaline (Ella) had prayed and turned to the bible for deliverance from her pain and suffering. She kept her "little red bible" at her bedside, reading, praying, fighting to live, hoping the Lord would save her.

*"O, lost, And by the wind grieved,
Ghost, Come back again."*

—THOMAS WOLFE, LOOK HOMEWARD, ANGEL

The night of Mayaline's death, I was all alone. I never received even a single call from my family members the night of Mayaline's death to help soothe my grief. I was sitting on my couch at home, in the dark, wailing, and horribly lonely.

I darted out of the door and stood on my porch, looking at the funeral home on the corner of my block. I thought of Mayaline all alone, lying on a metal cart in the cold morgue at the hospital's contracted morgue provider. Maybe, I thought, I can go there and be with her. They probably embalmed her body and this would be too painful for me to see. She wouldn't look like my mom even being a medical professional wouldn't make me brave enough to endure the sight. Yes, I could look at other corpses, but not my mom.

In my desperate state of mind, I wondered if they butchered her and took her organs to sell. What a foul thought, but I had just seen a movie where people were killed for their kidneys to be sold on the black market.

I came back inside, afraid that I would see a ghost walk out of the funeral home. That would be all I needed in my misery!

I went back in the house and sat on the couch again, never turning on the light, thinking about the only person Mayaline had in her life on her death bed... me. My best friend of twenty years worked in the Oncology unit my mom was on at the hospital. Not once did she come in my mom's room to even give her a sip of water. Amazing how friendships can come and go over the death of a loved one.

I decided to focus my thoughts on fond memories of Mayaline. Mayaline loved music, her happy melancholy lyrical salvation to soothe her lonely life in Chicago. I decided to go in the room where Mayaline had slept during her short stay in my home and play music on the stereo. I put on memorable CD's and played a mixture of dance songs. The volume blasted loudly, the walls vibrated, and I twirled around the room in a dance frenzy. I envisioned in my mind the picture of Mayaline dancing beside me when I was a little girl. She had a 70's go-go dancer's body: slim, tall and small hips, with a cute little butt.

1:00 a.m., I was exhausted. I thought, time to get some sleep. Tomorrow will sap my energy with all the to-do's related to Mayaline's death planning logistics.

I turned off the stereo, leaped down the stairs and dived into bed. I fell into a deep intensive sleep within five minutes. It's amazing but I've always managed to sleep despite what terror I had endured. I believe this to be a consequence of being a nurse. I always had unexpected havoc at the hospital, death or trauma events or a patient managing to find a way to commit suicide on the psych unit. I would come home and crash from pure exhaustion and sleep for twelve or more hours. Mayaline would warn, "You are going to get bedsores from sleeping so much."

I'd lash out and say, "Guess what mom, I had a miserable night at work." I could see her become tense and psychologically try to prepare her mind for what I was about to say. She hated hearing me depict graphic stories of hospital events, especially if we were eating dinner. "Maggots were oozing from a patient's foot wound and then his toes fell off on the floor, all black and oozing green exudate mixed with blood. I had to pick them up off the floor and put the toes in a plastic bag to be sent to the morgue for safekeeping."

She would immediately lose her appetite, stop eating and glare at me. If she had been capable of having knives shoot from her eyes directed at my heart, this would have made her elated. Then Mayaline would get up and leave the table. I would continue eating, giggling and euphoric over my conquer... pay back.

Around 3:00 a.m., the stereo I had turned off started to play, louder than I had the volume earlier in the night. The room was directly above my bedroom downstairs, so this music was right in my face. Frightened beyond plausible comprehension, I bolted and sat straight up in bed, thinking I was possibly dreaming. As I continued to listen, I realized that I wasn't dreaming. The music kept playing in the room above me, the last place that Mayaline had slept outside the hospital where she died. She never got to go to a home again.

I slowly creeped up the steps, as if I was ascending into the twilight zone. Spooked and tense, I rounded the corner to go into the room. The music was still playing rather loudly.

The blue psychedelic lights that surrounded the CD lit up in an eerily purple-blue neon glow, swirling. Kneeling in front of the stereo, my mind began to wander. Maybe I hit a pause button and the stereo was set to play two hours after I turned it off. I didn't see a pause button, but I had to imagine this to keep my sanity.

While kneeling in front of the stereo, I turned the stereo off. I had to turn and stand to get up, but I was frozen stiff in fear, scared that when I turned around I would see a spirit, Mayaline's or a menacing presence. This has always been my greatest fear. I stood and turned, no spirit... whew!

I ran back downstairs and got back into bed, my mind confused and my body aching from physical exhaustion. I hugged the pillow, imagining that this was my security blanket and I was asleep in two minutes.

Thirty minutes later, the stereo blared again, the same CD. I had two others in the stereo.

Now, terrified and extremely nervous, I creeped extremely slowly up the stairs, my eyes as wide as saucers. I envisioned that I was going to see a ghost at any minute and then would ultimately faint.

It was 3:30 a.m. Who could I call to explain this incident? Not the police. They would take me to the psychiatric unit and admit me as a 5150 bizarre case. The absolute answer: "No one."

I rounded the corner again, sweaty, and peered back in the room. Same scene as before: blue psychedelic lights in an eery glow, music blaring. This time, I turned off the stereo and quietly said, "Mom, you're scaring me."

In my apprehension, I thought she'd answer me back. I

waited for ten minutes. Nothing... quiet. For some odd reason, I didn't feel like bolting out the house. Where was I going to go. After about twenty minutes, I went back downstairs, almost crawling from pure mind and body strain. I turned the lights on, jumped into bed and pulled the covers over my head. The stereo didn't turn back on. I fell asleep.

The next morning, I awoke at 9:00 a.m. to the quiet and stillness of the house. As I put my foot on the first step of the stairs, I hesitated, thinking the stereo would start playing music. I could break into a sprint run into the garage, get in my car and bolt from the house. I waited for five minutes; no music.

Slowly, I creeped upstairs to make my morning coffee. As I landed on the top stairs, I turned and walked towards the room, looked in, and all was quiet. I slowly walked the hallway back into the kitchen, fearing the music will start playing loudly any second, but then were no further episodes.

I immediately decided to call my mom's favorite sister, Aunt Willie Bee, to tell her about the incident. After blurting out the series of sequences that occurred the night before, she calmly replied, "Maybe there was a short in the electrical wiring of the stereo."

"No," I defiantly blurted. My house is brand new, eight years old and I've never had this occur previously with the stereo. I play music from the unit constantly and I've never experienced such a bizarre occurrence.

She was quiet, no response.

After about ten-seconds of silence, we shifted the conversation to briefly discuss the upcoming funeral arrangements for my mom. Since we both started to cry, I told her that I'd call again in a couple of days. As I walked towards my office, coffee in my hand, I quickly peered at the stereo. It looked ominous after last night's bewitching and goosebumps rose on my arms.

At my office desk, I began the daunting task of calling Mayaline's insurance company and then the director of the funeral home to prepare for the burial.

Tiredly grinding out work all day, night approached like the creeping of fog in an alley. I exited my home office to collapse on the couch, relax and watch television. Listening to music while sipping on a glass of champagne sounded enticing, but I was horribly spooked about last night's events. I decided not to play my favorite CD selections on the stereo. For sure, if a faint lyric sound came emit from the stereo, I'd be sure to abandon the house and retreat to the police station. What a story to be told to the station clerk or cop! There was not a sound, and I slept peacefully through the night.

The following week, I decided to test the stereo just to make certain that the wiring was not faulty. The stereo turned on normally without incident. The harrowing incident that occurred the night of Mayaline's death the prior week never transpired again, or at least while I was home.

Four

Mississippi
The Magnolia State

Mayaline's embalmed body was flown back to Mississippi, her birth state. She was born in a little town named Utica. Mayaline's wish was to be buried next to her sister and favorite nephew. Arrangements had been made with the funeral director at the funeral home of previously deceased family members.

As I boarded the plane to fly to the funeral, I could hear music playing on the airport audio system. Suddenly, the song that had played repetitively from my stereo at home the night of Mayaline's death, roared from the speaker system. I sat down in my assigned seat on the plane, stared out the window and whispered to myself, "This is real."

Arriving in the "Magnolia State" was like a warp in time coming from San Francisco. Everything around there moved like a snail, unlike the hustle and bustle in the big city. Worse yet, put this state in the Big Apple, "New York City," and it would become extinct.

Rain poured horrendously two days before the funeral, and I nervously fretted over the thought that Mayaline's casket would be lowered into a muddy-water soaked gravesite. "The casket will mildew unless the soil is dry," I thought.

The heavens beamed with rays of sun streaks between the clouds on the day of the funeral and it appeared that the wetness just evaporated and the burial hole was satisfactorily dry.

Terry, the owner of the heavenly birds, was standing a few feet from the canopied burial site, dressed in a black business suit, white crisp shirt and a red tie. Besides him was a lovely white cathedral throne basket that housed the snow white feathered doves.

As Mayaline's casket was lowered in the moist ground, two beautiful, healthy doves were released into the air. They circled in the sky for about ten minutes and then disappeared from view. Remembering back to Psalms 55, verse 6 in Mayaline's little red bible, I felt at peace. Had I honored her wish that she circled in her bible before her death: "Was it meant to be?"

After the funeral, I said my goodbyes to the family and returned to the Bay Area.

The following month was Mayaline's birthday, May 28. She had been truly looking forward to turning 62. Her name was on the waiting list for the low-income senior housing building where her other sisters lived. Her eligibility to move in would have occurred that month, the year of her death, 2008. Strange, how life tragedies hit people at the most unfortunate times in their life.

I decided to take a trip to visit her gravesite and celebrate her retirement age birthday. How joyous and festive an event this would have been for Mayaline. I created a lovely, colorful spring mix with imitation flowers from Pier One and arranged them decoratively in a cone-shaped styrofoam flower holder. I bought a large duffle bag to put the flowers in as a carryon on the plane.

The day of the flight, I walked with a slow gait to enter the ramp heading to my assigned seat.

This time when I entered the plane's ramp corridor to fly back to the Magnolia State, not a familiar song played on the speaker system.

I immediately thought back to the time when Mayaline would call, and wish me well on my flight departures. Suddenly, in my train of thought, my cell phone rang. I immediately looked at the display on my cell phone and the number displayed was Mayaline's old cell phone number. It showed "Mom." I answered as if I was going to hear her voice, but there was no sound, just silence.

I had kept my mom's number in my phone as a gesture of remembrance of her existence. I thought, how strange?

Was she calling in spirit to say, "Goodbye" or I know you're coming to visit with me?" I'll never know and thank god I didn't hear that giggle and, "Are you flying my favorite aircraft?" Mayaline's voice on the other end of the phone line.

I landed in Mississippi, safe! I picked up my rental car and drove out of the airport, heading straight to the cemetery. It was 5:00 p.m., not dark yet due to the summer hours. To my physical discomfort, it was still hot with thick humidity, but not to the extent as if it had been twelve noon with the sun shining directly on you.

I decided to play the radio in the rental car and listen to songs and sing as I drove on the interstate. Familiar songs played that reminded me of Mayaline.There will always be songs that will be a remembrance of life, no matter what year.

I finally reached the cemetery and parked the car on the road a short distance from her gravesite.

I grabbed the flowers and started to exit the car. I screamed in utter delight, "Hi, Mayaline... I'm here to celebrate your birthday!"

A phone started to ring.

Startled, I checked my cell phone and no call was registered. The phone rang again, only once this time. I looked on the floor of the car, thinking maybe a prior renter had left their phone in the car. My check resulted in no phone found on the floor or in my immediate vicinity. Finally, I decided that I'd look again when I returned to the car thinking maybe I'd missed a crucial location.

Heading to the gravesite, I started to sing loudly, "Happy

Birthday." Since the headstone had just been placed a week before my visit, the vase was empty of flowers.

I carefully placed the colorful floral arrangement I had created in the new vase and then I took a picture.

After expressing my love, sorrow, regret, and saying the Lord's prayer, I walked back to the car.

As I got into the car, the phone rang again. This time I decided to call the rental car company to tell them that a phone was ringing in the car. The agent told me that a phone was embedded in the dash and to look for a phone key symbol. I did, and to my surprise, there was a button with a picture of a green colored phone symbol. I lightly pressed the button and the phone started to ring. A woman answered with a business voice. She announced, "This is KGOX radio station."

I suspiciously asked, "Who are you? Did you call the phone in this rental car?" I was erratic, terrified and out of my wits at this juncture.

She replied,"I didn't call the phone in your vehicle. I'm the disc jockey at the radio station and your call registered as coming in on our guest line."

I began to explain how I had received a series of phone rings in the rental car. Neither she, nor I could make any sense of the incident. I told her the situation was perplexing and at this moment there's no logical explanation. I ended with, "Goodbye, and thanks for listening to my rambling," and I hung up the phone.

I put the key in the ignition and became fearful that I would have another frightening incident. The car started and I let the vehicle idle for a moment, gripping the steering wheel with perspiring hands.

As I drove the narrow cemetery roads towards the interstate, the phone didn't ring as it had when I entered the cemetery about an hour earlier. It remained silent as I exited and picked up speed to 70 miles per hour on Interstate 405. Apprehensive, I decided not to turn my radio back on at this particular juncture.

En route to the hotel, my mind raced with the ghostly thoughts: "Was Mayaline's spirit communicating through the phone? Was she trying to let me know that she knew I was at her gravesite, or was it the music, the familiar lyrics in a song?" Spirits are forms composed of electromagnetic energy.

Restless and fidgety, I made an abrupt U-turn and headed back past the cemetery to drive forty-five minutes and visit a distant cousin in Vicksburg. I figured, the long drive would do me some good and help me clear the perplexed thoughts in my head.

Vicksburg was a remote and isolated country back roads town. I knew I would get lost driving and trying to find the home. I called my cousin as I exited the interstate and was relieved to hear that she'd send her husband to meet me so I could follow him to the house. I just remembered how dark it was and I was worried about finding my way back to the interstate. After a somber two-hour visit, it was time to leave and head back to my hotel before it got too late. I told my cousin I was afraid that I wouldn't find my way back to the freeway.

She replied, "It's a straight ten-minute drive, you'll be fine." If you get lost, call and we'll come lead you out of town back to the Interstate.

I replied, "I think I'll be just fine."

On my solo, boring drive back to the interstate, the phone in the car rang again as the green phone light illuminated in the dark. I hadn't seen this earlier at the cemetery because it was bright daylight and bright in the rental car.

I jumped, but focused on my driving along the narrow one lane road. This time I knew how to answer the phone ringing in the car. I pushed the green phone button and answered, "Hello?"

Silence...

I don't know why I wasn't afraid. I should have been scared out of my mind. Staying calm, I hung up the phone by pressing the phone symbol and then the color changed to red. I was praying that the phone wouldn't ring again. Then I'd really pass out at the wheel, which wouldn't be a good thing on this narrow country road.

I made it to the interstate and swore I'd never again visit my cousin at night, at least, not by myself. I pulled up at the hotel, and dashed upstairs to my room.

Once settled in bed, I focused on the day's events and all I could do was stare at the ceiling, exhausted. I began to think about the word "spirits." My mom had always worried when I drove late at night by myself, especially on unfamiliar turf. She always worried that I'd fall asleep at the wheel, because I'd go all day without resting. I believe she rang the phone in the car to alert me that she was there looking out for me. With this thought, I pulled the covers over my head and fell into another coma-like sleep.

The next morning I awoke early at 7:00 a.m. to eat breakfast at the cereal bar at the hotel, dress and get quickly out to the cemetery before the temperature reached 90 degrees, which would be in about two hours. Today I wanted to say, 'Happy Birthday" for the last time and then I'd leave for the airport to fly back to the Bay Area.

Entering the cemetery today was uneventful, no phone ringing in the car. It was 8:00 a.m. and the morning was peaceful and still, and the sun was shining brightly. I noticed that I was the only one at the cemetery.

In walking to the gravesite, the grass was wet with the morning dew. I reached the gravesite and I immediately started to sing "Happy Birthday." Then I knelt down and wiped off the wetness from the newly laid gravesite stone marker.

As I stood up, I noticed a section of the trees started to sway back and forth with a mild wind, directly to the right of where I was standing by the grave. What was so remarkable was that only a small section was moving, not the whole row of trees that extended the length of the cemetery.

I looked back at the pasture and saw that a few cows had gathered at the fence, staring in the direction of the swaying tree section, as if, like me, they thought, "How peculiar"

After about five minutes, the trees stopped swaying and the swooshing wind sound ceased. Out of the clear blue, a faint music started to play and then I heard crackling of branches and leaves in the direction of previously swaying trees. I peered closely and squinted my eyes to sharpen and focus my view to see if I could see a house beyond the blowing trees. All I could see was the woods that extended into never-never land and no home came into view.

I know it was probably just a squirrel scurrying about, but what explains the music? Maybe kids were playing in the distance and was carrying a boom box radio with them.

I started to pace back and forth, trying to come to grips with the recent occurrence in the wooded area. I shook off the incident, looked down at the gravesite and said my "Good-bye" until my visit for Mayaline's birthday in 2009.

Driving out of the cemetery, I looked in my rear view mirror to see if the trees in the isolated section by Mayaline's grave would start blowing again. Nothing quiet as when I drove in about two hours ago.

Driving down the interstate, I decided to track the trees to see if houses would appear alongside the interstate. None appeared until about five miles up the highway.

I know. Next time I'll just put on my hiking gear and hike in the area where I heard the music, crackling branch as leaves. How foolish. I knew this would be an impossible adventure, clearly ludicrous and insane. Squirrels or birds may walk on fallen branches and brown dried leaves, but music just doesn't play in wooded areas.

Mayaline had always hated my interactions with the non-reliable beauticians I had to patronize based on my high profile executive position and career. She would always comment, "Cut it off, then you don't have to interact with those crazy females." I would always protest I didn't want to cut my hair and that I'd eventually one day locate a reliable stylist I could work with one day.

Driving to the drug store one day to pick up a prescription, I saw a sign announcing a new beauty shop that had opened in my neighborhood. "Bingo!" I yelped.

Curious, I parked and entered the shop. I was greeted by a quirky girl named Frankie, who stated she'd welcome the opportunity to service a new client. With that, I made an appointment and was sitting in her beauty chair the following Saturday.

Extremely pleased after my visit, I made another appointment for a Saturday again in two weeks.

One week before my appointment, I received a call from Frankie informing me that she was put out of the shop by the owner.

I asked, "Where do you plan to go?"

She replied, "I'll have to do hair at my home until I find a new shop to rent a space for my clients." I agreed to have my hair styled at Frankie's home the next Saturday.

Frankie's home was not conducive to performing hair care appointments. The house was not tidy and reeked of stale cooking grease. A makeshift corner on the kitchen table was the styling area, with a hair dryer parked in the middle of the floor.

In casual chatter, she mentioned that her boyfriend was laid off and always asleep in the back room. I managed to be polite and let her finish my scheduled service. Despite my dissatisfaction with the daunting makeshift salon, I compromised and made an appointment for the next Thursday.

Thursday approached quickly! As I parked and walked to the door, I noticed a light on in the bedroom. The rest of the house was pitch black dark. I knocked and got no answer, so I called Frankie's cell. It just rang. Puzzled, I got back in my car and waited for ten minutes.

Upset and disappointed, I started my BMW 525 and drove slowly away, still hoping that Frankie would notice me. To my surprise, as I peered over my shoulder to glance quickly at the house, the bedroom light flickered off.

Weird...

As I drove two blocks the other way, I ended up in a cul de sac and was lost. Looking up at the street signs, I saw the name of my mom "Ella," and the other sign that crossed that one, had my deceased cousin's name "Rita." How strange, I said to myself? This is a rarity. I was such in awe that I stopped the car, got out and took a picture of the street signs with my cell phone.

Then all of a sudden, I saw two opaque white circles the size of tennis balls. They began to circle around each other. I knew my headlights were not playing tricks on me, because the tennis ball objects were brighter than my headlights. "Orbs," I whispered to myself. I've read about and seen pictures of what I was staring at in several metaphysical magazines. I would have never imagined that I'd be staring at these mystical spiritual transformations.

"Orbs" is a sign that the spirit is there to offer protection to the people in the area. White energy is typically perceived as positive in nature. In reading the book entitled, "The Orb Project," two leading scientific experts in the field of the orb phenomenon combine their years of knowledge to examine these ghostly apparitions.

The orbs photographed in the book are referred to as "Spirit Emanations," spirit being "itself" or just an emanation from it. Both would lead to the same conclusions that spirit beings are:

- All around us.
- Highly evolved and intelligent.
- Capable of changing their size and location extremely quickly.

We can summarize these conclusions in one important statement: Photographs of spirit emanations offer evidence as close to scientific proof as we have ever come in proving the existence of the spiritual reality that, "Divine Presence" is real.

Sensing the orbs were a sign of protection and a warning, I decided to keep driving and to never contact this beautician again.

The remainder of 2008 had to be the loneliest period in my life, depicting a twilight zone of humanly existence on planet earth. Orphaned without a mom, dad, sister, brother or close family ties, the reality creeped in to disturb my psyche.

"Happy New Year" 2008 is here.

An advertisement in a medical journal read, "Body Scan $299.00, will detect any signs of cancer."

"Hypochondriac" was my middle name, so I decided to have the body scan at a local hospital.

On the day of the scan, I went to the radiology section of the hospital to register for the scan with the coordinator named Liza. After completing the paperwork, Liza escorted me to the elevator to take me to the X-ray department.

As we entered the elevator, the doors closed and we started to ascend. Within a few minutes, I started to smell a putrid odor of acid smoke. I turned to Liza and asked, "Do you smell that smoke?"

She replied, "No."

When the elevator doors closed as we exited and we started to walk towards the X-ray department, I no longer smelled the smoke.

Protective spirits can manifest as a smoke smell. Mayaline was on that elevator to be with me, concerned for my safety and well-being. She had traveled many trips to the X-ray department to have CT scans done. She feared this huge, noisy machine and the procedure. I recall walking next to her while she was on the gurney going to the x-ray room and as the orderly steered the gurney into the room, she started to scream and cry uncontrollably. Witnessing this act of desperation just broke my heart and I began to whimper. I wiped her tears and hopelessly stated, "Don't worry, Mom, the physician just wants to see what the cancer is doing inside your body. I'll be right here in the waiting area. Be brave like you are, no worries."

My scan results were negative. "Whew," what a relief.

One year after. It was time for me to fly to the "Magnolia State" and celebrate Mayaline's birthday again.

Mississippi was hot and humid, as usual for this time of the year. As I turned off of Highway 205 into the cemetery, I noticed I was the only car in the whole cemetery, but it was only 8 a.m. Great timing to beat the heat.

The Garden Memorial Cemetery was flat and open, trees surrounding the grassy grounds. One could see all the graves with flat headstones while driving along the small concrete driveway.

I parked my car and walked over to Mayaline's grave with a floral spring mix in my hand to place in the vase. As I raised the metal vase to clean the water that collects in the hole, the most beautiful Monarch butterfly flew out of the vase opening and landed on my cheek for a second and then flew up and circled around Mayaline's grave.

Christianity considers the butterfly as a symbol for the soul. The butterfly is depicted on ancient Christian tombs and Christ has been illustrated holding a butterfly in Christian art. Could it be that Mayaline's soul was released in this butterfly from the confines of her body in the casket several feet below? I thought of the Hopi prayer:

"Do not stand at my grave and weep.
I am not there, I do not sleep
Of quiet white doves in circled flight
I am the soft stars that shine at night
Do not stand at my grave and cry
I am not there, I did not die."

I decided to take a cell phone picture of the colorful Monarch continuing to circle around Mayaline's grave. It was a breathtakingly rare and cherished moment.

As I looked at the picture, I noticed a thick white hazy cloud had formed around Mayaline's grave, with the Monarch resting on the tombstone. I thought it must be the settings in my cell phone, so after about five minutes I took the picture again. This time the haze was not apparent in the second picture and apparently the Monarch had flown away, slipping out of my eyesight since I had focused my energies on the photo in my cell phone.

I closely studied the first photo. "Strange," I mumbled to myself. It looks as though a ghostlike form was hovering over the grave. "Could this be feasible?" I asked myself.

Another orb presence, "Spirit Emanation?"

If this was the case, surprisingly, I wasn't spooked, just in a state of bewilderment and awe. "Mayaline?" I thought... "Mom?" Walking to my vehicle, I looked back and waved, "Goodbye."

After I left the cemetery, I drove to my Aunt Glenda's house and told her about the remarkable butterfly and photo incident. She just stared with her mouth wide open, no speech.

To break the silence, I reminded Aunt Glenda that we needed to turn in early to get a good night's sleep for our drive to Memphis in the morning. The purpose of the trip was to visit my elderly Uncle Blue who was just tossed in a nursing home by his younger aged spouse. When we called Uncle Blue a few days ago, he was yelling and crying in the phone, howling that he wanted to go home and be with his wife.

Unfortunately, we didn't get a chance to leave until 11 a.m. the next day. My Aunt Glenda decided not to help drive since the gout in her knees had flared up over night. The thought of my driving three hours there and back made me furious, but I was destined to see Uncle Blue. This might be my last visit, one never can harvest time.

Arriving in Memphis and walking into the nursing home, the first sight in the corridor by the nurses station was Uncle Blue standing up in his wheelchair with the safety belt around his waist, apparently trying to get loose.

When he noticed us walking down the hall towards him, he started crying and screaming. Witnessing this brought tears to my eyes.

After visiting and saying our farewells, I knew I'd probably never see Uncle Blue alive again.

It was nighttime when we were heading back to Jackson. I was tired, sleepy and almost about to have an accident due to exhaustion when a butterfly quickly flashed in front of the windshield and lingered for about two minutes. I immediately thought of her, my mom, "Mayaline." She hated when I over exerted myself and if family contributed to this exhaustion, she'd become horrifically furious, having highly elated tantrums.

I screamed out load to my aunt, "Did you see that butterfly?"

My auntie, napping next to me, suddenly opened her eyes in a groggy stupor and grunted, "Huh?"

I replied, "Never mind, it's nothing, just go back to sleep and rest."

I continued to stay focused on the windshield hoping the butterfly would return.

The butterfly never returned and I continued driving in the night, eyes heavy and burning with fatigue. I felt as though I had a wavering energy field that kept me awake and focused on the road. For if I closed my eyes, then I'd be asleep and an accident would be sure to occur. We made it home, without incident, "Thank Heavens."

As I dozed off to sleep, I thought of the butterfly, since butterflies don't fly at night.

This one did...

January 2010, "Happy New Year." The Super Bowl, Martin Luther King's Birthday and mine, special occasions for this month every year.

Feeling lonely and isolated, I decided to try online dating again. I swore I wouldn't after the encounter with the monster a few years back, but I definitely couldn't count on an eligible suitor walking up to my door with flowers and a box of chocolates announcing, "I'm the one!"

One evening I was engaged in a phone text with a potential date named George. He mentioned that he had a great dinner with his mom. This statement crushed my heart, since I'll never be able to enjoy and eat another dinner with Mayaline, my mom.

Then George texted, "My mom is so special to me."

I thought, so was mine and then I blinked away tears from my eyes.

After saying our texted goodbyes by way of our phones, I slouched on my leather sofa, pouted and seethed with anger that others had their moms.

After about thirty minutes, a text came through my phone. I looked and it was George's number, but no message appeared in the text box.

One minute later, George's number came through again and I looked for the text. Again, no message.

I thought, *maybe George forgot to write a message in each text*, so I texted him back with "Message?"

He responded, "What?"

I texted, "You just sent me two texts with no messages."

He texted back, "No, I didn't."

I texted back, "Sorry to bother you, maybe it was a mistake on my part. Have a great remaining night."

Then I looked at my phone again, thinking, how silly, only to see that the texts were real with blank messages.

What's so perplexing is that two came through consecutively to signal that a crucial point had to be communicated.

Mayaline...my mom, wishing she could eat another dinner again? Was she warning me about this new online guy?

Web of Lies...

Two weeks before my birthday, I became fixated on a rather large billboard that one sees as they enter San Francisco on the Bay bridge. This billboard sat high above the bay bridge, looming into view. It had a new movie announcement. I couldn't help but notice the date was depicted in large print and read May 28.

Eyes widened in disbelief, I whispered, "Mayaline's birthday. What a coincidence!" I drove into the city everyday, same route so I would always notice the billboard and date.

May rolled around again and I was in Mississippi for my annual visit to Mayaline's grave to celebrate her birthday.

Two days before Mayaline's birthday, I started to think about how my mom played the "Daily Lotto" almost everyday with the hopes of winning a little money. No thoughts of becoming rich, just a little bit more than what she received from her disability checks. The amount wasn't enough to live on in the big city of Chicago.

She would call me and say she just got home from riding the bus to play the daily lotto at the corner store.

I decided to call my Aunt Willie Bee in Chicago to remind her of Mayaline's birthday this year. While on the phone, I casually mentioned that for the first time in my life, I had seen a rather larger billboard hovering above the Bay Bridge as I entered San Francisco, displaying the numbers of Mayaline's birthday.

I reminded my aunt how Mayaline played the daily lotto, and she said that she remembered those days since Mayaline would call her if she hit the jackpot. Mayaline would be besides herself when she won fifty dollars. I told my aunt to play the three numbers on Mayaline's birthday, 5, 2 and 8.

May 28 rolled around as quickly as a ball on a roulette wheel. The two of us forgot to play and the "numbers hit."

Was it a coincidence or a "Morse Code from Heaven?"

My excuse, I was at the gravesite putting flowers on the grave and singing, "Happy Birthday."

Returning home from Mississippi, I buried myself in my work, achieving above average performance. Despite this achievement, my relationship with my manager and teammates was strained and counterproductive.

June, time for the company's semiannual employee-wide meeting in Florida.

At one of the break out-sessions with my team members, my manager rudely confronted me in front of the team. I felt embarrassed and humiliated.

It was a rather warm and pleasant day in Orlando. The French doors in our meeting room were wide open leading to the outside and the patio. The goal was to have fresh air in the room.

Suddenly a flock of white birds hovered outside the door, squealing rather loudly and frantically flapping their wings, so fierce that feathers were flying everywhere. A wind blew up out of nowhere and then a distinct burning smell of smoke entered the room. My teammates commented,"What is going on?"

After about ten minutes, the birds flew away, and the burnt smoke smell faded and eerily all was quiet. Instantly, I knew, Mayaline's spirit was present, to signal, "I know, stay strong."

I decided to go shopping at the resort later that evening. In the store, I glanced up at an item that had my mom's name on it... "Ella."

Mayaline had a habit of giving money to family members who were saddened by adverse events in their life. Her favorite currencies to give were the two and twenty dollar bills. As I walked down an aisle, I saw a crumpled green colored piece of paper on the floor. Blinking to focus on the item, I squatted and picked it up.

"Oh my gosh, it was a twenty dollar bill." I sighed and thought of Mayaline and her twenties.

Ring, ring... "Hello." My Aunt Glenda called to say she was going to the cemetery to put flowers on the graves for Thanksgiving holiday.

Elated, I replied, "Please call me when you get to the gravesite."

She called when she reached the gravesite.

I happily shouted in the phone, "Happy Thanksgiving, Mayaline, my beloved Mom."

Aunt Glenda came back on the phone and proudly spoke about how gorgeous the flowers were in the vase on Mayaline's grave.

All of a sudden, a distant, scratchy sounding voice intercepted the line. Confused, I held the phone tighter to my ear. "Hello, Auntie are you there?"

The eerie raspy voice spoke again, but I couldn't make out the words to formulate a sentence. The voice reminded me of what one would hear on those ghost programs when the paranormal team audio taped a ghost or spirit talking on their specialized equipment.

No specialized equipment here. I heard this familiar ghost sound aired on those television shows through my own phone line.

"Hello?" I stated again. Now silence.

I decided to hang up and I immediately called my Aunt Glenda back. She answered.

My voice shaking, I yelled, "Where did you go?" I was calling your name and a scratchy, eerie sounding voice came on the line. Did you hear what I heard?" I asked.

"No, I was calling to you and I couldn't hear you either. Something weird did happen while I was trying to hear your voice back on the line. The radio in the car abruptly turned on, roaring loudly out of nowhere but, I didn't turn it on."

"Wow! What the hell just happened?" Spirits in the cemetery.

"I'm driving like a bat out of hell from the cemetery and my body is ridden in goose bumps," my Aunt whispered in a low tone.

"Me, too" I commented. "Call me when you get home."

After I hung up the phone, I sat quietly and whispered, "Mayaline."

Feeling antsy after the Thanksgiving paranormal experience, I decided to book a last-minute trip to visit Mayaline's grave for the Christmas holiday. I decided to create a festive, colorful silk Poinsettia flower arrangement to place in Mayaline's vase. I called my aunt Glenda to let her know that I'd be in town for the Christmas holiday. She was thrilled and stated, "Now, I have a reason to cook a festive holiday feast. I told her that I was flying in on the day before Christmas Eve and I'd be heading straight to the cemetery to place the flower arrangement in Mayaline's vase.

I remembered the twenty dollar bill that I had found on the floor of the shop after seeing "Ella," my mom's name.

I was going to give Mayaline her favorite two dollar bill as a Christmas present.

The plane landed and I immediately jumped up once the seat belt light went out. I grabbed the Polo duffel bag from the overhead storage and checked the flowers, hoping they were not smashed due to other passengers jamming items in available carry on storage space.

I sighed with relief, they were still perfect.

As I drove to the cemetery, I was nervous that some sort of strange occurrence would happen. I entered the open gates and drove slowly to the back of the cemetery where Mayaline's grave was located.

At 6 p.m., I was the only visitor in the entire cemetery.

I walked to Mayaline's grave from my vehicle. I kneeled and carved out a piece of the grass sod and then placed the tightly folded two dollar bill in the soil. I found some loose dirt and saturated the two dollar bill with the dirt to ensure it would never loosen. Then I placed the grass sod back over the two dollar bill.

I thought to myself, there's no way this two dollar bill will ever surface; it'll be my personal secret for years.

Satisfied, I then placed the lovely flower arrangement in the vase.

In a festive tone, I sang,"Merry Christmas, Mayaline. I gave you your favorite two dollar bill as a gift." Relieved that I didn't hear a reply, I got in my car and drove out of the cemetery.

I decided to go directly to the hotel from the cemetery to get some shut eye. I'd spend Christmas Eve and Christmas Day with my aunt, and then fly back to California to enjoy New Year's Eve with friends.

My Aunt Glenda called me on New Year's Eve to let me know that she had gone to the cemetery to visit Mayaline's and her son's grave, which was located 20 steps in front of my mom's grave. She stated that, to her surprise, "A dry two dollar bill was lying neatly on her son's headstone."

"Oh," I gasped.

She replied, "I'm dumbfounded that money would be lying on my son's grave, and of all imaginable things, a unique two dollar bill!"

Who put it there and why? I wondered.

I told her my secret of what I had done when I visited Mayaline's grave on the day before Christmas Eve.

I then whispered, "What if?" and then I just became silent and so did my aunt.

In my own precious thought I wondered, what if Mayaline's spirit connected with her favorite nephew and she passed on the two dollar bill? In the past, she always gave her nieces and nephews two dollar bills as special monetary gifts.

The year 2011 rolled in as normal. Another "Happy New Year!" per the traditional holiday slogan. At the start of the New Year, I became interested in the subject matter, "Soul existence of the deceased."

I located several articles on the subject, and the majority of the findings concluded that the soul can make its presence known, especially to loved ones, through electronic devices or taking the form of anything on planet earth.

Could it have been Mayaline's spirit in the CD player at my home the night of her death, trying to find her way in her new existence or spiritual form? The paranormal incident at the cemetery summoned my curiosity to embark on a quest to research religions that honored the spirit of the soul.

The ever so famous Internet can be a wealth of information to search titles and find information on topics. I came across an interesting spiritual ceremony that remembered deceased loved ones.

"The Lantern Floating Ceremony," held annually on the island of Waikiki in Hawaii and hosted by the Shinnyo-En Buddhist organization.

This festive ceremony brings together more than 40,000 visitors from around the world who set afloat lanterns at sunset over the Memorial Day weekend in remembrance of loved ones who have passed, or as symbolic prayer for a harmonious and peaceful future.

The lantern floating provides a venue for many people to celebrate and reconnect, beyond the boundary of life and death, with the lives of those who transitioned to a spiritual realm, and to offer heartfelt appreciation to those who passed. Many participants write names of their lost loved ones on lanterns and float them on the water with their prayer of love, sorrow and appreciation.

The Shinnyo-En belief: "Our ancestors gave lives to their children and they then gave lives to their children. This infinite connection of lives has brought each of us to be here today. When we deeply comprehend the meanings of this connection, we naturally come to find our profound appreciation to our past (our ancestors) and preciousness of our lives. This recognition gives us a higher aspiration to fully live every present moment, and it inspires us to build a better world for future generations."

I envisioned that a temple must exist in my area. Low in behold, one was located near my home. I decided to attend a service and learn about the ancient traditions of Shennyo-En Buddhism.

The following Sunday, I was attending a service, what a unique experience. At the end of the service, the congregation worshipers had an opportunity to create their own message for the upcoming Lantern Floating rite. What a lucky day for me! The parchment paper would be taken to

Hawaii by one of the leaders at the temple in exchange for a small donation.

I wrote my message to Mayaline and included her favorite picture on my designated piece of parchment paper.

I located the temple leader who would be attending the event in Hawaii... Eveline was her name.

I introduced myself to Eveline and informed her that I was sending my message with hope that the parchment paper would be included on one of the lantern floats in the ocean. She stated that there's no way she'll know for sure, since volunteers would be assembling the lanterns with hoards of messages from all over the world.

"No worries, I'm sure all will be superb." I told her to have a safe trip and I'll see her when she returns from the ceremony.

The week after the Memorial Day weekend, I ran into Eveline at the scheduled Sunday temple service.

Her eyes wide, she blurted, "You wouldn't believe the fascinating occurrence on my first day at the event.

I was walking around the area where the volunteers were assembling the thousands of messages on the lanterns to prepare them to float that evening. The first one I saw is the one you sent in memory of your mom."

"Amazing," I replied. "Her spirit wanted you to see this and tell me, don't you think?"

Eveline whispered in my ear, "I agree."

"Thou body ceased function and succumb to death in my fight.

My spirit will roam and I'll be with you in this form of my new life."

I had been plagued with a series of unsettling dreams since the start of the year. In every dream, I was in a large supermarket and a shadowy figure would be pushing a cart shopping for food. In one of the dreams, the shadowy figure spoke about looking for the bakery section to buy sweets.

Without a doubt, I recognized and knew the voice to be that of Mayaline, my mom. Mayaline practically lived at the supermarket. She went every day and would call me complaining about the hoards of people scurrying about and the long lines at the checkout. As a result of her frequent shopping, she never had enough money, so I gave her a credit card to buy food or any item in the store.

I despised setting foot in a supermarket and would literally cry when I had to go and shop for food.

In an instant, I awoke and found myself in a seizure-like state, unable to move and my body shaking uncontrollably, then the episode ceased.

This scared me, so I went to see a Neurologist and he ordered a CT Scan and an EEG of the brain. The results were negative for both tests, my brain function was normal.

In September, the dream returned and in this dream, several deceased family members were in the store with Mayaline. This time when I awoke, my heart was beating and thumping as if I was about to have a heart attack. I stayed calm, hoping the intense palpitations would cease before I called 911 for an ambulance.

My heart calmed after about five minutes and I jumped out of bed thinking, "My heart was about to arrest." Full of fear and unsettling thoughts, I decided that it's time for divine intervention.

After work the next day, I made an effort to visit a large cathedral in the San Francisco area. The church always put me at ease and the gothic architecture made me feel grandiose and secure. After kneeling and praying at the Jesus statue hanging on the cold, grey stoned wall, I lit candles in every public section in the church in memory of Mayaline.

To my dismay, darkness had fallen and I had to trek three blocks up hill to my parked vehicle. I started to walk with my head down deep in thought about recent life and work related events. I felt safe since I walked alongside the church and not on the other side of the street.

As I completed one block, I heard a strange dragging noise. Abruptly, I looked up and saw an elderly women who appeared to be in her eighties coming towards me with a walker.

She appeared to be quite overweight and struggling with trying to walk with the walker.

Strange, I thought, it's too late for such an elderly woman to be out and about this time of night. I looked around and no one else was in sight, just her and me. It was eerily quiet except for the sound of the walker dragging on the concrete.

I slowed my gait and watched the woman, she never looked up and had her head down while she walked and struggled with the walker.

After about fifteen minutes we were beside each other, and then she looked up and directly at me. To my horror, when I looked at her eyes, none were visible, only two black holes.

I screamed and broke out in a run up the remaining hill to my car, never looking back at the woman. As I was running, I noticed I couldn't hear the walker dragging, so she had to be stopped in place.

I hurriedly jumped in my vehicle and locked the door, breathing and panting heavily, trying to catch my breath. I decided to drive back down the hill towards the eerie woman to see what direction she was walking and what house she would enter. When I reached the bottom, she was no where in sight.

I circled numerous blocks, knowing she couldn't disappear that quickly, it was only five minutes to my car and back to the spot where we had come into contact. Dumbfounded and scared out of my wits, I wonder what had I just seen, a ghost? The church did have a section of cremated remains in the attic area of the cathedral, and I was the last person to leave the massive structure.

To remain sane, I immediately forgot about the incident and drove home to finally sleep after a long day. The eerie image stayed on my conscience until I fell into a coma-like sleep from pure exhaustion, especially contributed to the nighttime incident at the church.

When I awoke the next morning, I thought about last night, confirming to myself that I didn't imagine what I saw. The figure had black holes as eyes. Who and what was this individual, creature or apparitions? I've never seen a ghost in my life. Maybe Mayaline in another form? My mind wondered back when Mayaline was trying to walk with a walker in the rehabilitation center and I recalled her legs being so wobbly, unsteady and in a severe form of ataxia. She cried out in anguish and my heart sank into my stomach. I tried to coach her by saying, "Hang in there Mayaline, you'll walk again one day." After consulting with her cancer physicians, she commented, "It wouldn't be so bad that she never walks and confined to a wheelchair, at least she'll be alive." I agreed and the following week, called a construction consultant to build a ramp at my house. This would never become a working project.

I shook the incident off and focused on the fact that November and Thanksgiving was right around the corner. Time to get prepared for the holiday season festivities, cooking for parties and bringing food for potluck events at friends' homes.

I had to go to the mega supermarket near my home to pick up a few items that I had been was out of for two weeks because of my defiant attitude about going to supermarkets. I realized I absolutely needed to go in order to prevent spending fifteen dollars a day on fast food for major meals.

Paper towels was on my list and a necessity, since I had been using toilet paper to wipe down my kitchen counter and to clean. I only use one brand of paper towels that was extremely pricey, but well worth the price due to its durability.

I had been pushing the shopping cart back and forth in this large market looking for items, and my knees started to hurt with excruciating pain. While in the bakery section, I cried since I knew that I had to walk back to the other end of the supermarket to grab my last item, paper towels. I called my mom's name and chuckled while stating out loud, "You know how I hate this place."

As I began to push the cart to head to the other far end of the store for the fourth time, I felt the urge to look to my right where a table of red velvet cakes were displayed for a Thanksgiving buy. A six-pack of paper towels suddenly appeared on top of the cakes, my special pricey brand.

I didn't recall them sitting there when I looked on the table of red velvet cakes a few minutes ago.

I had contemplated buying one, but I decided not to since I figured I'd eat the whole cake with milk in three hours.

I put the towels in the supermarket cart and headed to the check-out. "Mayaline, is your spirit wandering in this supermarket and made it possible for the paper towels to be there for me?"

The dreams, possibly if you believe...

Christmas a few weeks after Thanksgiving.

I had to call the florist in Mississippi to order my annual Christmas flowers that they delivered and placed in Mayaline's vase on her tombstone. The owner, Franco, was always dependable and would have the order completed in two days. I paid ten dollars extra to have a picture snapped by Franco's cell phone and he'd email me a copy of the picture for me to see his creative artificial flower design.

As with previous years, if I was driving in my vehicle, the "Mississippi song" would blast from my car radio. "Mississippi moon, won't you keep shinin' on me."

Then I'd know... I would rush home to check my email, and sure enough, there's Franco's email with the attachment. The flowers had been delivered.

This strange phenomenon has occurred since Mayaline's death in 2008.

After seeing the festive photo, I decided to take advantage of the time to print labels for my Christmas cards. As I opened my address document on my computer, I became saddened when I looked at my two aunts addresses who lived next door to each other in the senior citizen building located in a quiet and safe Chicago neighborhood.

It should've been three living in the same hallway, apartment numbers 103, 104 and 105, the latter being Mayaline's unit.

With this train of thought, I heard my fax/printer/copy machine turn on with a click and then a fax ring. The display started to light up with the neon blue color and the word "Receiving" blinking continuously.

I jolted up and ran over to yank the phone cord out of the wall. In horror, I glanced down and saw that the phone cord was not attached in the jack in the wall. I knew this, because every day telemarketers would call all day, so I made it a point to always disconnect the cord from the wall.

So, how is the fax working? I never touched the machine.

I slowly sat back down in my high-back cushioned Tempurpedic office chair, waiting to see if a paper with a message would print and discharge from the feeder.

As the white boxes in the neon display kept going back and forth, I tensed, waiting for the piece of paper to erupt. Then the machine cut off. No fax message presented in the holding tray.

I had braced myself in my office chair to expect the unknown phantom document. "What the Hell" I thought.

After this harrowing episode, I shut down my computer, closed the door to the office and decided the Christmas cards would have to wait until the next day or two, maybe even next week. What had just transpired in my office? Perhaps Mayaline's spirit in agreement that she wish she was living to be in the apartment, too.

Another New Year! It has been four years since Mayaline's death.

I decided that I'd start the New Year off by getting a roommate to ease my loneliness. Pictures needed to be taken of my spare room to post on websites for advertisement of the space. Since using the camera in my cell phone would allow for an instant download to my email, I decided this was the most viable solution.

It was an overcast day, but there was enough light in the room to capture clear photos. I took pictures of the wrought iron day bed, chest, treadmill, desk and the 42-inch television.

In reviewing the pictures, one caught my eye, the picture of the television. Right in the middle of the photo was a white circle, the size of an egg. I thought, "How weird, there's no light on in the room and I didn't turn on the flash on the cell phone camera." I decided to take another picture of the television. In this camera shot, no white circle. An Orb. Mayaline's spiritual orb. This was the last room that she called home before dying in the hospital. Could it be that her spirit always lived in this room or periodically, like NOW?

After experiencing several spiritual scenarios with Mayaline's soul or mysterious bonding connections, I embarked on another project to explore research about this phenomenon.

For the sake of knowledge and truth, I luckily found a novel entitled "Light after Life: A scientific journey into the Spiritual world," by distinguished author, Dr. Konstantin Korotkov.

In reading, I located several interesting paragraphs in the book as outlined below:

1   "Extra-corporeal" states, well known, especially in occult literature, and occurring in recent years with increasing frequency to ordinary people, not otherwise related with occultism. However, these states tell us almost nothing about what goes on with the soul after death other than it continues to exist and to have a conscience."

2   "The sphere where the soul goes in the beginning, upon first leaving the body, is not the heaven or hell, it

is a region close to earth, referred to by various names: 'other side', 'bardo plane' (Tibetan Book of the Dead), 'Realm of the Spirits' *(Swedenborg)*."

—HIERMONK *(SERAPHIM ROSE)*~ORTHODOX CHURCH.

3   "The main achievement of recent years has been the fact that the medical doctors studying the problem of resuscitation have supported the Christian teaching on the life of the soul. The first step, which is also the most important one, has been irrevocably taken: after death of the body, life continues. This fact has been confirmed by the medical science as well as by theology." (Kalinovsky, 1991)

4   All doctrines are agreed that there exists a tie between one's earthly life and the one's afterlife of the soul, and the latter is the continuation of the former on a different level.

The main objective of the book includes generalized information on physical and chemical changes occurring in the body during several days after death. It is now the domain of a specific science, "Thanatology." The author and his fellow researchers proved that the "soul lives." His experiments immediately showed that the deceased bodies exhibited a specific "Kirlian glow intensity," variable in time, but no qualitative difference existed between the discharge glow of the living and the deceased. The results of the experiment discovered a correlation between the type and cause of death, and the characteristic associated with the particular subject.

Three groups were classified and evaluated. Of course, this classification and, hence the existence of some typical, nominal ways in which the soul departs from the physical body.

1 "Calm, natural" death caused by the condition of body tissues.

2 "Violent" death, e.g., as a result of a traffic accident, with brain injury.

3 "Unexpected" death as a result of some tragic circumstance which could have been avoided in more favorable conditions.

Mayaline's fate closely resembles group three, since her exact cause of death is not one of the experimental subjects in the book.

"Group three," showed that 72 hours after death, the most intensity, high amplitude and duration of oscillations compared with the previous groups. The first 24 hours had an enormous "Kirlian aura glow." It peaked at night from 9 p.m. of various rate and duration. Local glow drop at the end of the first day and a sharp drop at the end of the second day.

Semion Kirlian, a Russian foreman who repaired medical equipment, accidently found this enigmatic glow. At the very beginning of his work, Kirlian was surprised to find that the electric crown around the fingers changes the color and size depending on the psycho-emotional condition.

The question that was raised in the very beginning of the experiments was: "What is the meaning of increased overnight activity in the deceased?" The phenomenon was observed on the first experimental night. In the morning, the night shift experimenter, a regular employee of the organization, noted a few things:

"Throughout the night, I felt the presence of a substance."

"What's that?" I asked, not understanding him. "Presence of what?"

"Substance. So we call the meandering spirit of the dead man. At nights and on weekends, it is usually much stronger than by day. This night, particularly, the substance was felt especially clearly."

On the next night the sensation was repeated only once, at 3:00 a.m.: on the third night there was absolutely nothing.

Skeptic if what the employee had experienced, the author (researcher) decided to check everything himself in the third experiment, a suicide case.

It is 11:45 at night. I come from the laboratory and along the deserted staircase, down to the basement. It is absolutely quiet in the building. Somewhere in the distant rooms there are guards and my colleagues.

I am alone.

Passing by the morgue, I come to the lower basement, and along the corridor to the door of our experimental room. Even in the daytime, the main denizens down here are rats.

I feel nothing but an empty room. The subject is at the distant end from the door, about 20 meters away.

I begin to move slowly ahead.

I reach the middle of the basement when suddenly I feel someone's glare directed at me.

Everyone has experienced this sensation, the pressure of someone's gaze on your back in a crowd, a store or a bus.

I come to the subject and turn on the equipment. The sensation is that someone is lingering nearby, watching all my actions. There is no hostility in this presence, only quiet observation. Quiet, but not indifferent.

It is not fear I feel, but rather the kind of discomfort you experience in unpleasant company: the sense that you're not wanted here.

Finishing the experiments, I turn off the equipment and leisurely go back to the door.

Here, the sensation of someone else's presence is absent. I once again slowly tour the room. Ah, here it is again!

I return to the distant end of the basement near the back of the wall, about three meters from the gurney with the body.

Here the sensation is present but not strongly.

Eventually I manage to determine that the presence is most intense approximately in the center of the room, some 5-7 meters from the body.

Then I headed for the exit.

This time, I feel a gaze on my back until the very moment I exit.

Only after closing the low iron door, I realize how tired I got over these last twenty minutes.

The author recounts that the increased nocturnal activity is probably significant. Absence of activity in the daytime cannot be attributed entirely to the influence of daylight, or to the greater number of people present: our basement room had no windows and was kept at a darkened level of illumination around the clock.

However, both sensations and the experimental curves demonstrate increased nocturnal activity.

Taking a breath from reading, I find myself gravitating to Mayaline's red Asian trunk that I bought in 2008 to protect her most precious keepsakes. I was astonished to find a 1970's branded Polaroid camera. I thought, "I wonder if this is valuable?"

At the very bottom, to my surprise, there's the Walkman that Mayaline so LOVED. I examined the condition, as I hadn't opened the trunk in five years. I pressed play, and no sound. I thought, "Oh no." It's broken. "No," I said to myself. "Maybe the battery is dead."

I opened the compartment and took the battery out. White corrosive substance was on the battery and inside the battery chamber. The white matter had also run onto the tape.

My heart sank in despair, thinking the tape was ruined. It was a classic, old TDK D90 tape.

I decided to put another battery in and the Walkman unit still didn't work. I thought, "Dammit, it's broke and this was Mayaline's most treasured item."

I decided not to give up, and I was determined to make the unit work, so I removed the battery and blew inside the battery chamber to get rid of some of the white matter, and then I wiped the white corrosive matter off the tape.

I picked another brand of battery, put it in the unit, pressed play and "WALLA." The music blared in the headphones!

This time I listened to the whole tape and realized that Mayaline had recorded all love songs on the tape. A mixture of blues, '70's and '80's songs, plus rhythm and blues classics!

Mayaline was God's creation of Love, for she loved everyone and so wanted to be loved again by a special mate. She was in the prime of her life when she died, and still an amazingly gorgeous woman.

I recall buying her an elegant bra and panty ensemble for a birthday present in 2007. She called me and said, "I have no one to wear this lovely set for and show it off."

Surprised, I stated, "One day you will, keep the faith."

I know she found him in Heaven!

~ I'm waiting for that Morse Code confirmation ~

REFERENCES

Light After Life: a scientific journey into the spiritual word. 1998, Dr. Konstantin Korotkov.

The Orb Project: to those who search for an understanding of reality and our place in it. 2007, Miceal Ledwith and Klaus Heinermann.

9780990344308